exploring

PUBLICATION
DESIGN

exploring

PUBLICATION
DESIGN

Poppy Evans

Australia • Brazil • Japan • Korea • Mexico • Singapore • Spain • United Kingdom • United States

Exploring Publication Design
Poppy Evans

Vice President, Technology and Trades SBU:
Alar Elken

Editorial Director: Sandy Clark

Senior Acquisitions Editor: James Gish

Development Editor: Jaimie Wetzel

Marketing Director: David Garza

Channel Manager: William Lawrenson

Marketing Coordinator: Mark Pierro

Production Director: Mary Ellen Black

Senior Production Manager: Larry Main

Production Editor: Thomas Stover

Editorial Assistant: Niamh Matthews

Cover Design: Steven Brower

For product information and technology assistance, contact us at
Cengage Learning Customer & Sales Support, 1-800-354-9706

For permission to use material from this text or product,
submit all requests online **www.cengage.com/permissions**
Further permissions questions can be emailed to
permissionrequest@cengage.com

ISBN-13: 978-1-4018-3147-9

ISBN-10: 1-4018-3147-8

Delmar
Executive Woods
5 Maxwell Drive
Clifton Park, NY 12065
USA

Cengage Learning is a leading provider of customized learning solutions with office locations around the globe, including Singapore, the United Kingdom, Australia, Mexico, Brazil, and Japan. Locate your local office at
www.cengage.com/global

Cengage Learning products are represented in Canada by Nelson Education, Ltd.

To learn more about Delmar, visit **www.cengage.com/delmar**

Purchase any of our products at your local college store or at our preferred online store **www.cengagebrain.com**

Printed in China by China Translation & Printing Services Limited
5 6 7 14 13 12

contents

Publication Design Within an Historical Context

An introduction to publication design would not be complete without an understanding of the origins of written and visual language and how printing technologies have influenced publishing and publication design. This chapter focuses on these aspects as well as designers who have influenced recent trends in publication design.

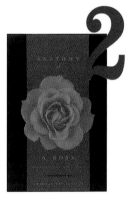

The Principles and Elements of Publication Design

Publication design is a process of applying basic visual principles to create order and visual interest in a publication. This chapter presents an overview of the principles and elements of design and how they are applied to publications and in support of a communication goal.

Using Color Effectively

This chapter addresses color and color psychology and discusses color systems and their application in publication design and production. Principles that create color harmony and unity are also explored.

Understanding Type 74

Page Layout 94

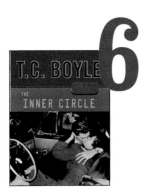

Imagery 120

CONTENTS

INTENDED AUDIENCE

Publication design requires a basic understanding of design principles and a knowledge of how to apply them to a multi-page format. *Exploring Publication Design* explains how these fundamentals work when applied to magazines, books, annual reports, promotional brochures, newspapers, newsletters and catalogs. The text is supported with professional examples and custom diagrams. Additional chapters discuss the history of publishing and publication design as well as career opportunities for designers in the publishing industry. *Exploring Publication Design* is intended for intermediate- to advance-level design majors and design professionals needing information specific to publication design.

BACKGROUND OF THIS TEXT

Although many resources exist to help designers in their understanding of design fundamentals and typography, few are devoted to publication design. Other books serve as showcases for examples of great publication design, but fail to explain how underlying principles make these examples so effective. *Exploring Publication Design* was created to address the unique challenges involved in designing within a multi-page context by examining successful publications and the visual processes and psychology that are the basis for their success.

TEXTBOOK ORGANIZATION

Readers are introduced to publishing's history at the beginning of the book. From there, they learn how fundamental design principles are applied to publications. The book ends with an overview of career opportunities in publication design.

Chapter 1 is devoted to an introduction to publishing within an historical context. Readers get acquainted with the origins of written and visual language, how changes in the industry and evolving technologies have influenced publishing and publication design, and find out who has influenced publication design trends.

In Chapter 2, readers are given an overview of the basic elements and principles of design and how they are applied to publications. This chapter also addresses how design works in support of a communication goal as well as the importance of creating hierarchy and harmonious spatial relationships in a layout.

Chapter 3 addresses color and color psychology and includes information on how to create harmonious color combinations. This chapter also covers how color works as a unifying element in a publication and the role of color systems in publication design and production.

Chapter 4 is devoted to typography. Typographic terms and measurement systems are discussed as well as typeface classifications. Readers learn how to select typefaces that are appropriate to a project's design and communication goals and discover ways that type can lend expression to a design.

Chapter 5 discusses page layout and how grids work to provide structure, unity and flow in a publication. This chapter also provides more in-depth information on how design principles apply to type in a layout and how to effectively combine typefaces, assign hierarchy, and combine type with imagery.

In Chapter 6, readers develop an understanding of imagery's role in publication design. by learning how to appreciate the differences between photography and illustration and how they can most be effectively be applied in publication design.

Chapter 7 addresses the importance of format in publication design and how size and color can support a publication's communication goal. This chapter also discusses the importance of selecting the right type of binding and paper and how a publication's design can aid navigation and readability.

Chapter 8 shows how design fundamentals are applied to specific examples of publication design. Readers are presented with case studies that explain how typography, color, and other design elements and principles work together to produce a magazine, newspaper, newsletter, annual report and promotional brochure.

In Chapter 9, career opportunities in publication design are explored. The qualifications and demands common to most publication design jobs are discussed as well as the differences between specific areas of publication design. Readers also learn about the work and careers of successful publication design professionals.

FEATURES

The following list provides some of the features of the text:

- Shows how the fundamental principles of design apply in the specialized field of publication design.
- Showcases award-winning examples of publication design, deconstructing them to reveal underlying design principles at work.
- Profiles successful publication designers, offering revealing insight into the careers of working professionals.
- Features engaging and entertaining sidebars that bring a fresh and enlightening perspective to the book's content.

SPECIAL FEATURES

Objectives

Learning objectives start off each chapter. They describe the competencies the reader should achieve upon understanding the chapter material.

Sidebars

Sidebars appear throughout the text, offering additional valuable information on specific topics.

The Designer At Work

These career profiles, located within chapter nine, allow the reader to learn from the example of successful designers who have won recognition in the field. Samples from their award-winning portfolios are included.

Review Questions and Projects

Review Questions and Projects are located at the end of each chapter and allow readers to assess their understanding of the chapter. Projects are intended to reinforce chapter material through practical application.

E.RESOURCE

This guide on CD was developed to assist instructors in planning and implementing their instructional programs. It includes sample syllabi for using this book in either an 11 or 15 week semester. It also provides chapter review questions and answers, exercises, PowerPoint slides highlighting the main topics, and additional instructor resources.

ISBN: 1-4018-3151-6

ABOUT THE AUTHOR

Poppy Evans is Assistant Professor of Communications Arts at the Art Academy of Cincinnati, where she has been teaching since 1994. Her background includes experience as a graphic designer and magazine art director, as well as serving as Managing Editor for *HOW* magazine.

Over the past 15 years, Poppy has written hundreds of articles for design publications such as *HOW*, *STEP*, and *Print* magazines. She has authored or co-authored fifteen books including *Forms, Folds and Sizes*, a production manual and reference guide released in 2004. She has served as a board member for AIGA Cincinnati and is the recipient of many awards for both her design and writing.

Photo by Eric Soderlund

ACKNOWLEDGMENTS

Many thanks to the designers, illustrators and photographers who contributed their work to this book, as well as the following individuals whose work, expertise and mentoring contributed significantly to my understanding of publication design and design education: Ruth Britt, Lori Siebert, Gregory Wolfe, and my colleague, Mark Thomas.

Many thanks as well to my students who have contributed so much to my knowledge during my teaching career and who continue to challenge me to grow and learn. I would also like to thank Jacob Grant who developed diagrams for this book.

Thanks to my Delmar, Cengage Learning team of professionals who offered support, ideas and guidance: Jim Gish, Jaimie Wetzel, Thomas Stover, and Niamh Matthews. A thank you also goes to Jeff Somers at Graphic World.

Delmar, Cengage Learning and the author would also like to thank the following reviewers for their valuable suggestions and expertise:

Scott Carnz
Assistant Dean of Academic Affairs
School of Design
Art Institute of Seattle
Seattle, Washington

Lorrie Frear
Graphic Design Department
Rochester Institute of Technology
Rochester, New York

Nathan Gams
Graphic Design Department
McIntosh College
Dover, New Hampshire

Nancy Rorabaugh
Graphic Design Department
Art Institute of Atlanta
Atlanta, Georgia

Poppy Evans
2005

QUESTIONS AND FEEDBACK

Delmar, Cengage Learning and the author welcome your questions and feedback. If you have suggestions that you think others would benefit from, please let us know and we will try to include them in the next edition.

To send us your questions and/or feedback, you can contact the publisher at:

Delmar, Cengage Learning
Executive Woods
5 Maxwell Drive
Clifton Park, NY 12065
Attn: Graphic Communications Team
800-998-7498

Or the author at:

poppy@one.net

seventeen

JULY 1949 · 25 CENTS

| publication design within an historical context |

1

objectives

Understand how written language and publishing evolved over time.

Appreciate how changing technologies have affected publication design.

Learn about important publication designers and how they have influenced the development of publication design.

introduction

Simply put, publishing means communicating with people. The word is derived from the Latin word *publicus,* meaning "belonging to the people."

Although publishing originally meant to make publicly known, it now refers to the preparation and dissemination of written material for public consumption. Publishing today differs from other types of public communication (e.g., the internet, broadcasting), in that it involves words and pictures within a printed, multipage format. Publication design involves the organization of content and arrangement of words and pictures within this context. Books, magazines, and newspapers are types of printed literature that we come into contact with every day.

From Primitive Communication to the Printed Word

To understand how publishing and publication design came about, it helps to be aware of the history of graphic communication, or communicating with words and pictures. Graphic communication dates back to the beginning of human history, when prehistoric men and women used cave paintings of animals, human forms, and symbolic shapes and patterns to depict hunting scenes and other events in their lives. (See Figure 1-1).

Over time, these images evolved into written language. Early civilizations devised a language in which imagery was reduced to a more simplified pictorial representation called *symbols*. The earliest known writing systems made use of these pictorial symbols or *hieroglyphics*. Hieroglyphic scripts appeared in Mesopotamia, Romania, Iran, and Egypt around 3000 BC. The Chinese, Mayan, and Aztec peoples also developed primitive hieroglyphic writing systems.

However, it was the Egyptians who were most remarkable in their efforts to evolve a writing system that used hieroglyphics to represent words and sounds. Their sophisticated writing system consisted of more than 500 symbols or characters. The Egyptians were also able to progress in their graphic communication beyond previous, more primitive cultures by painting their hieroglyphs on papyrus, a form of paper. Many historians believe that the Egyptians were the first people to produce manuscripts that combined words and pictures. (See Figure 1-2).

At about the same time, Near Eastern civilizations were developing their own written language called *cuneiform*. Cuneiform script was inscribed on clay, stone, metal, and other hard materials and evolved over a period of time, from pictograms to a linear style better suited to inscription on clay. By the second and first millennia BC, cuneiform was impressed into tablets of wet clay

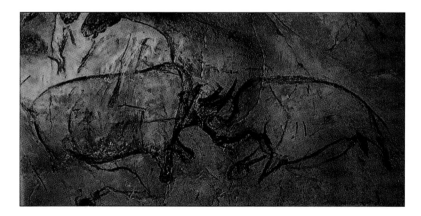

Figure | 1-1 |

Although there are no wholly satisfactory theories as to the meaning and interpretation of cave paintings, their crude imagery gives us an awareness of what was important in the lives of the primitive cave dwellers who made them. (Image from Chauvet cave, Australia, courtesy of *Time* magazine.)

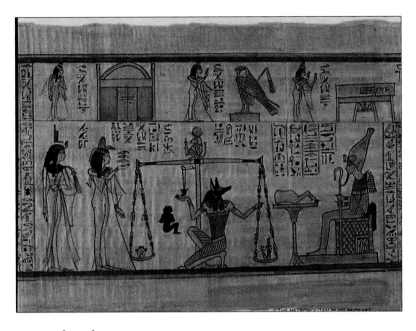

Figure |1-2|

The ancient Egyptians produced early manuscripts by painting imagery and hieroglyphic symbols on papyrus, a form of paper.

with a reed stylus. These tablets, sun-dried or baked in kilns, are important records of ancient Near East cultures. (See Figure 1-3).

The scholars and writers of Phoenicia (the ancient Greek name for a narrow coastal strip of Palestine-Syria) reduced the cuneiform script used by the Assyrians to a collection of 22 characters. This advancement accomplished two things: it condensed written language to a manageable number of characters and converted its abstract symbols into a more linear format. The Greeks later adopted the Phoenician system to create their own alphabet. In fact the word *alphabet*, is derived from the first two Greek characters—*alpha* and *beta*. The Romans, who borrowed extensively from Greek culture, further refined the Grecian alphabet to 21 characters that closely resemble the alphabet we use today. (See Figure 1-4).

original pictograph	later pictograph	early Babylonian	Assyrian	
				BIRD
				FISH

Figure |1-3|

Over time, cuneiform symbols evolved from pictograms to more abstract symbols. As they evolved, the symbols were rotated from a vertical to a more horizontal orientation.

Semitic Phoenician	Semitic Phoenician	Roman Early Latin	Today
✕✕✕	ΛΑΑ	ΛΛ	A
ϽϽϽ	ββΒ	ββ	B

Figure | 1-4 |

Typographic letterforms evolved over time, from the Phoenician alphabet to the letterforms we know today.

During medieval times, graphic communication was rarely available to anyone beyond the ruling class, bishops, and religious scribes. These scribes produced early Christian doctrines called *illuminated manuscripts*—elaborate and highly detailed books that combined words and images with decorative letterforms. They were painstakingly written by hand in gold, silver, and vivid pigments and then handbound into large volumes. Pages were originally crafted from vellum, a very thin sheet of calf or sheep skin, but were later produced on paper made from rags. The most popular illuminated books were large Bibles and psalm books, which were mostly assembled for wealthy merchants, the nobility, and the monasteries. (See Figure 1-5).

Publishing Comes of Age: Renaissance to Industrial Revolution

As Europe grew out of the Middle Ages and into the Renaissance, mass production of the printed word became possible due to the efforts of Johann Gutenberg, who is credited with the invention of movable type. Gutenberg, a German goldsmith by trade, developed a process of crafting single letters from brass and then casted them in molten metal. Text was created by assembling these letters onto a flat printing surface, which Gutenberg then inked and imprinted onto paper with a converted wine press. Gutenberg, who also developed an ink that would adhere to his metal type, is widely acclaimed for printing a Bible on his crude press. The printing process Gutenberg invented,

Figure | 1-5 |

Illuminated manuscripts were highly detailed religious books that were painstakingly written by hand by religious scribes during medieval times.

CHAPTER 1

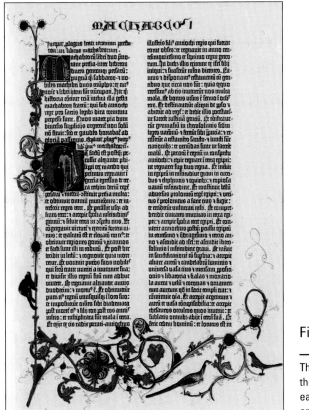

Figure |1-6|

The typeface Gutenberg designed for his 42-line *Bible* replicates the pen-drawn letter styles popular in Germany at the time. This early publication serves as testament to Gutenberg's ability to create beautiful typography as well as timeless design.

called *letterpress*, came into common use in Europe after his death in 1468, and helped to spread knowledge and enlightenment through the printed word. (See Figure 1-6).

As publishing flourished in Europe and England, typography evolved into letterforms that more closely resemble the roman typefaces we work with today. Early roman typefaces were designed in Venice by the French printer Nicolas Jenson during the 1470s. By the middle of the sixteenth century, type designers such as Claude Garamond were integrating Renaissance ideals of proportion into their typeface designs.

By the eighteenth century, type foundries were abundant throughout Europe and Great Britain. One of the best known was founded by British typographer, William Caslon. Caslon's type was just as highly regarded in colonial America as it was in England. In fact, the first printed version of the Declaration of Independence was set in Caslon, a font of his design.

The letterpress method of printing is also still in use. Letterpress is a printing process known as "relief," meaning that type and imagery is on a raised surface that receives ink. Areas falling below the surface of the printing area, do not receive ink and are not printed.

Letterpress printing has been refined and perfected over the years. By the mid-nineteenth century, it had become automated (powered initially by steam) and was widely used for printing newspapers, handbills, and other literature. Advances were also made in the paper-making process during this time. By the end of the nineteenth century, electronically powered presses, printing on paper fed from a continuous sheet or roll, were generating 20,000 complete papers in an hour.

Letterpress is used today by artists and designers who love its antique quality and the debossed impression it leaves on paper. Its commercial applications are typically invitations, announcements, stationery and other small-run jobs not requiring four-color process. (See Figure 1-7).

Gravure is another form of printing that has its roots in fifteenth-century Europe and that is also still in use today. Gravure is the commercial form of *intaglio* printing, a process that involves etching an image onto the surface of a plate which is then inked and wiped clean, leaving ink only in the recessed areas. When printed under pressure, the paper draws the ink out of the engraved areas, transferring the image onto paper. Gravure has evolved over the years to accommodate multicolor printing at high speeds; it is preferred by

Figure |1-7|

The letterpress method of printing evolved from Gutenberg's original invention of applying ink to metal type. Although this printing method is still in use today, many of today's letterpress artisans have replaced metal type with metal plates made from computer files. (Photo of Tom Strassel from the Cincinnati Museum Center.)

those who seek a high grade of image reproduction. Gravure and rotogravure are mostly used today for printing postage stamps and publications in extremely large quantities.

In the late eighteenth century, another printing process called *lithography* was invented by the German playwright Aloys Senefelder. Lithography (which means "stone-writing") is based on the

Figure |1-8|

In the late nineteenth century, lithography was used to print posters by French artists such as Henri de Toulouse-Lautrec. (Image of *Divan Japonis* courtesy of Digital Image © The Museum of Modern Art (Licensed by SCALA/Art Resource, New York)

principle that water and grease do not mix. Ink is applied to a smooth, flat surface, such as a metal plate or stone, on which the image to be printed is ink-receptive. Because ink is oily, applying water to the blank areas of the surface makes them ink-repellent. Lithography grew during the nineteenth century as a means of printing color and imagery, and was used widely for printing posters, newspapers, and magazines. (See Figure 1-8).

Although letterpress and gravure continued to be popular methods for printing in the first half of the twentieth century, in the past 50 years *offset lithography* (the commercial form of lithography) has become the most often used method for printing publications. The term *offset* comes from the process of transferring an image to a rubber-covered blanket cylinder, which then transfers that image onto paper. The discovery of the offset process happened quite by accident when Ira Rubel, a New Jersey lithographer, noticed that when a feeder missed a sheet on his rotary press and the impression was made on the cylinder, the back of the sheet next to go through the press took the impression from the cylinder. Offset lithography was born when Rubel devised the first offset press in 1905.

Publishers favored offset lithography as a method of printing over letterpress, intaglio, and gravure for several reasons. A chief advantage is that the rubber blanket cylinder prints uniformly on all kinds of paper. The lightweight "litho" plate was also a much more convenient and economical substitute for the heavy type and lock-ups used for letterpress.

Offset presses today range in size from one-color presses that print on individual sheets of paper to large multicolor web presses that print on paper from rolls. These presses run at high speeds and are so efficient that they can print both sides of the paper simultaneously, generating hundreds of impressions per minute. (See Figure 1-9).

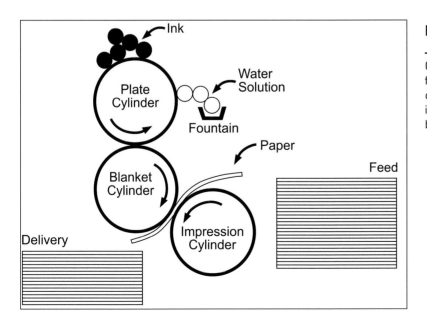

Figure |1-9|

Offset lithography is based on transferring an image that is inked onto a plate cylinder to a rubber blanket cylinder. The image is transferred from the rubber blanket onto paper.

Figure |1-10|

When a continuous-tone black-and-white image is made into a halftone, it is converted to a series of dots. The dots are large and close together in the darkest areas of the image, and they are smallest in the highlights.

The advent of photography in the nineteenth century also had a profound impact on graphic communication and publishing. Most credit Daguerre with photography's invention with his introduction of the daguerreotype in 1839. However, the ability to reproduce a photograph in detail did not occur until 1880 when *The New York Graphic* printed a *halftone reproduction* of a photograph on its front page. The *halftone process* further revolutionized publishing by allowing printers to convert continuous tone imagery into a series of black-and-white dots. (See Figure 1-10).

By the end of the nineteenth century, full-color reproductions were possible by an extension of the halftone technique that involved using camera filters to separate an image into four printing plates, one each for each of the four process colors.

Twentieth Century Graphic Reproduction and Design

The ability to print type has evolved rapidly in the past 100 years. Although the hand arrangement of metal type as part of letterpress printing continued well into the twentieth century, other methods of mechanical typesetting also came into use. In the early part of the century, linecasting machines, such as Linotype, increased efficiency over hand-set type by allowing users to cast lines of type, called "slugs," rather than individual characters. Similar systems, such as Ludlow and Monotype, came into use at about the same time.

As technological advances made typesetting and the printing of color and imagery much easier, publishing began to flourish. The early half of the twentieth century saw American magazines such as the *The Saturday Evening Post* and *Harper's Bazaar* evolve as opportunities for photographers, illustrators, and designers to showcase their work. Magazine art directors such as Alexey Brodovitch, who served as art director for New York City-based *Harper's Bazaar* from 1934 until 1958, forged new territory with magazine layouts that incorporated lots of white space and type as shape. A Russian immigrant, Brodovitch incorporated the work of prominent European artists and photographers in his layouts, commissioning work from Salvador Dali and Man Ray, among others. (See Figure 1-11).

After World War II, New York City developed even further as an influential design community. Artists, photographers, and other creative professionals thrived on the advertising and publishing generated within the city. Within this community, designers such as Bradbury

Figure | 1-11 |

Alexey Brodovitch, art director for *Harper's Bazaar* from 1934 to 1958, often formatted type into lyrical shapes as demonstrated in this layout where text is configured to echo the shape of the figure in the photograph. (Magazine spread courtesy of *Harper's Bazaar*, New York, NY. Photograph courtesy of the Walker Art Center, Minneapolis, MN. Photographer: Hoyingen-Huene)

Thompson made their mark on the industry by introducing new imaging techniques and innovative typographic treatments. Thompson's work was featured in a series of brochures published by Westvaco and showcased the color reproduction capabilities of the paper manufacturer's coated stock. (See Figure 1-12).

New York City-based magazine art directors also established themselves as important influences within the design community. One of them, Cipe Pineles, made major contributions to editorial

Figure | 1-12 |

Working with a limited budget, Bradbury Thompson developed innovative ways of working with type and found imagery to create visual interest. His designs for *Westvaco's Inspirations* introduced experimental typographic techniques and explored the potential of using eighteenth- and nineteenth-century engravings as illustration.

Figure |1-13|

The designs of Cipe Pineles, who served as art director for *Glamour*, *Charm*, and *Seventeen* magazines, was characterized by an appreciation of color, pattern, and form, as evidenced in this cover design from 1949.

design during the 1940s and 1950s, initially as art director for *Glamour* and later at *Seventeen*, *Charm*, and *Mademoiselle*. Pineles' contributions were acknowledged by the New York Art Director's Club, which broke with its all-male tradition when it admitted her to membership in the 1940s. (See Figure 1-13).

Otto Storch, a student of Andre Brodovitch, made his mark on magazine design in the 1950s and 1960s. As art director for *Better Living* and later *McCall's* magazines, Storch was one of the first art directors to create expansive layouts that showcased eye-catching photography. (See Figure 1-14). Another of Brodovitch's students, Henry Wolf, became art director of *Esquire* magazine and developed a new format for the publication that emphasized photography and white space. When Brodovitch retired as art director of *Harper's Bazaar* in 1958, Wolf took over, experimenting with typography and inventive photographic layouts. (See Figure 1-15).

Figure |1-14|

Otto Storch used the expansive format of *McCall's* magazine (10½ × 13 inches) as an opportunity to feature large-scale photographs. He often featured ordinary objects treated in unexpected ways in his layout.

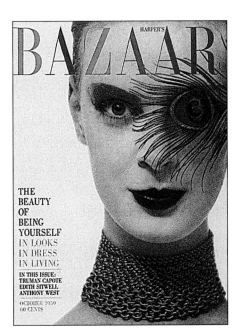

Figure |1-15|

As art director for *Harper's Bazaar*, Henry Wolf was known for inventive photographic concepts such as this arresting image in which a juxtaposed peacock feather simulates the model's eye makeup.

In the 1960s, phototypesetting revolutionized the publishing and typesetting industries by providing a fast, flexible, and inexpensive means of setting type. Phototypesetting was also the ideal typesetting method for offset lithography, which was rapidly replacing letterpress printing. Phototypesetting machines allowed type to be projected onto paper or film, which was then pasted down onto a board along with imagery and other graphic elements. In addition to being more efficient and economical, it was also an affordable means of producing type in-house, giving designers more flexibility to format and adjust type themselves. This flexibility created an opportunity for greater typographic expression, perhaps best exemplified by the work of Herb Lubalin, a New York City-based designer and art director who made significant contributions to editorial design during the 1960s. (See Figure 1-16).

Among the publications Lubalin art-directed and designed were *Eros*, launched in 1962 as the "magazine of love," and *Fact* magazine, which featured exposés of hallowed institutions. At the end of the 1960s, Lubalin became art director of *Avant Garde* magazine. The logotype Lubalin designed for *Avant Garde* was developed into a typeface with the same name. Lubalin designed other fonts as well. (See Figure 1-17). During the 1970s, Lubalin became increasingly involved in type design and became design director for International Typeface Corporation (ITC), which was, and still is, a major supplier of fonts.

Figure |1-16|

Herb Lubalin's knack for typographic expression is apparent in this design for a magazine logo in which the ampersand enfolds and protects the "child."

The most phenomenal impact on typography and design was yet to come. In the early 1980s, personal computers such as the Apple Macintosh gave designers even more control over the typesetting process by allowing them to manipulate type and create their own typographic designs. The computer allowed designers to reshape

Figure |1-17|

One of the fonts Lubalin designed, Avant Garde **(left),** originated with the *Avant Garde* logo **(right),** shown here on a title page for *Avant Garde* magazine from 1969.

letterforms, layer type, configure it into shapes and curved paths, and otherwise make it conform to a designer's concept in ways that it had never been made to conform before. (See Figure 1-18).

The computer also allowed designers to conceive, develop, and market their own computer-generated typefaces by making them into keyboard-accessible fonts. Zuzana Licko of *Emigre*

Figure |1-18|

The layered and jumbled type David Carson created in th late 1980s and early 1990s gained high visibility in *Beach Culture* and *Ray Gun* magazines. These typographic effects were much easier to create on the computer than with photo-typesetting or earlier methods of producing type.

magazine pioneered this movement with the introduction of her font designs in the late 1980s. Dissatisfied with the limited fonts available for the early Macintosh, Licko used her fonts in the publication of *Emigre*, a magazine she developed with partner Rudy VanderLans that quickly became a design lab for digital technology. The pixelated, digital look of Licko's typefaces had fresh appeal for a design industry that was just beginning to switch to computerization. (See Figure 1-19).

In the early 1990s, the popularity of *Emigre's* typefaces inspired other designers to create and sell their own digital fonts. Today, the convenience of marketing fonts over the internet has offered even more type designers the chance to make their typefaces easily accessible as downloadable digital fonts. Well-known digital type foundries that are flourishing today, such as House Industries and T-26, were founded by designers during this era.

Computers also gave designers a chance to manipulate and work with imagery in new ways. April Greiman was one of the earliest designers to do this with photographic collages she assembled on the computer. Greiman's brand of "hybrid imagery" repeated and layered photographs and graphic elements in ways that were previously unattainable with traditional methods. (See Figure 1-20).

In addition to giving designers total creative control over typography and imagery, the computer revolutionized the way publications and other printed projects are designed and produced. Before the computer came into common use, designers would create a pencil or marker rendering

Figure |1-19|

Founded in 1984, *Emigre* magazine celebrated design culture and new technology with its incorporation of early Macintosh fonts designed by Zuzana Licko. Because of the limited resolution available at that time, Licko's early typeface designs were pixelated.

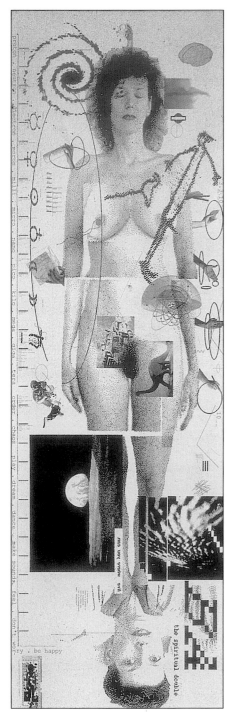

of a design, and then produce a "paste-up" or "mechanical" with type and imagery placed on different layers of acetate. The completed mechanical was sent to a commercial printer where a series of film negatives were made from each of the layers of the mechanical. The process was labor intensive and used far more materials than today's methods. Furthermore, designers were not able to fully realize what a printed piece looked like in color until a proof was made from these film negatives. Creativity was often inhibited by the inability to visualize alternative approaches to a design as they were being conceived.

Computerization has also facilitated the design and production process by allowing designers to easily share their ideas with others by transferring digital files over internal networks and the internet. It has also made publishing a possibility for less affluent societies and for many individuals who are finding that they can produce and distribute literature more cost efficiently than ever before. At one time publishing was an option that was only available to those with money and power. State-of-the-art technology has made books, magazines, newspapers, and other types of published literature more plentiful today than at any other time in our history.

SUMMARY

Publishing as we know it today involves combining words and pictures within a multipage format. Graphic communication, or communicating with words or pictures, dates back to prehistoric times when cave paintings of animals and other imagery were used as a means of nonverbal expression. Over time, these primitive images evolved into simplified pictorial representations or symbols. Early civilizations developed written languages based on these symbols. These hieroglyphic forms were further refined by the ancient Romans into an alphabet that closely resembles the one we use today.

Figure |1-20|

This foldout poster by April Greiman was included in a 1986 issue of *Design Quarterly*, published by the Walker Art Center in Minneapolis. It features image layering and digital imagery acquired from data disc and videotape, including earth-from-space photographs supplied by NASA.

During the Middle Ages, religious scribes produced early Christian books called illuminated manuscripts. During the Renaissance, publishing really came of age with Gutenberg's invention of movable type and the printing press in the fifteenth century. The printed word helped spread knowledge and enlightenment throughout Europe and Great Britain, bringing an end to the Middle Ages. Gutenberg's method is still in use today through a process called letterpress. Other printing methods, such as gravure, lithography, and halftone reproduction, were developed in the nineteenth century and allowed artisans and publishers to print black-and-white and color imagery. By the twentieth century, publishing was becoming a thriving industry. Magazines gave many designers an opportunity to showcase their capabilities. A flourishing design community developed in New York City, spawning many great and influential editorial designers. The invention of phototypesetting in the mid-twentieth century put typesetting and type design in the hands of designers, offering greater opportunity for typographic flexibility and expression. However, the invention of the personal computer in the 1980s has had the biggest impact on publication design. Computerization has streamlined the production process and given designers even more design flexibility.

in review

1. What role did symbols play in early written communication?

2. What is cuneiform and how was it used?

3. What form of written communication existed during the Middle Ages?

4. How did Johann Gutenberg influence publishing?

5. What is gravure?

6. What form of printing was used most often from the 1600s to the early 1900s?

7. What is offset lithography?

8. What role did Cipe Pineles play in editorial design?

9. How has phototypesetting affected publication design?

10. What role has the computer played in publication design?

notes

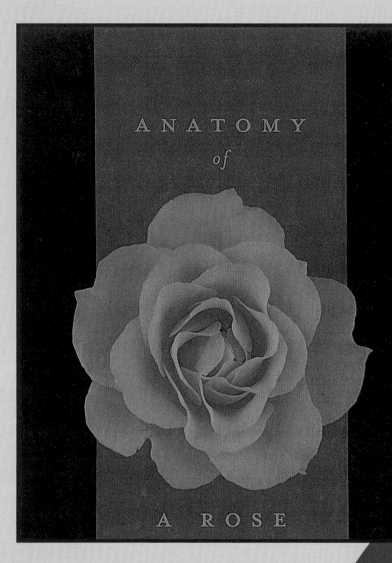

| the principles and elements of publication design |

2

objectives

Learn how a publication's goal, audience and other considerations determine its design.

Understand how basic design principles dictate how to work with design elements in a page or cover layout.

Understand how the elements of design operate as components in a page or cover layout.

Develop a basic understanding of how to organize design elements and create harmonious spatial relationships using proportional systems and grids.

introduction

Design is a visual language built on fundamental principles and elements. The elements (shape, line, and color) are governed by principles or rules that create order and visual interest or appeal. A publication designer works with these design principles and elements and combines them with words (in the form of type) and imagery to achieve a publication's purpose or goal. The goal may be to inform, persuade, sell, or entertain. The designer's role is to manage the design process in an informed way by fully understanding the publication's goal and how it can be achieved using the principles and elements of design.

This chapter focuses on the importance of understanding and interpreting a publication's communication goal as well as the basic principles and elements of design as they are applied to publication design. You will also learn about ways of directing eye movement in a layout and organizing visual content in ways that are visually engaging and harmonious.

Communication and Design

Design is basically giving form and visual meaning to a publication, based on its purpose. But before the design process can begin, it is necessary to have a full understanding of a publication's goal, its intended audience, and where it will be seen and read.

Understand the Goal

Publications are conceived and developed for any number of reasons. However, the *goal* of most publications can be broken down into four categories. Publications exist to (1) *inform*, (2) *persuade*, (3) *sell*, or (4) *entertain*.

1. Inform: This textbook was conceived as an instructional aid for students who want to learn about publication design. Simply put, the goal of this book could be stated as "help students learn how to design publications." In addition to textbooks, other publications that educate or inform include instruction manuals, newspapers, encyclopedias, dictionaries, and directories.
2. Persuade: Publications that persuade try to convince the reader to make a decision or act in a deliberate way. Examples of persuasive publications include campaign literature, travel brochures, and other promotional literature that persuades its audience to buy or invest in a product or service.
3. Sell: Sales literature is different from persuasive publications in that it serves as a sales vehicle. Publications that sell allow the reader to see merchandise, make informed choices, and then follow through with a purchase. Catalogs, for instance, allow a reader to read about, select, and order merchandise.
4. Entertain: Publications that entertain include novels, comic books, or any other publication that exists solely for the purpose of entertaining the reader.

Although some publications have just one goal, many publications have more than one goal. For instance, magazines contain useful information, provide some entertainment value, and include ads that attempt to persuade the reader to buy advertised products and services.

Identifying the primary goal of a publication is the first step in conceiving an effective design approach. (See Figure 2-1).

A good way to be sure you understand a publication's primary goal is to put it in your own words. Write it down on a piece of paper to be sure you can articulate it.

Know Your Audience

Another crucial component in the design process is understanding a publication's target audience and how to design in a way that will appeal to this audience. The target audience is the group of individuals to whom a publication is directed.

Figure |2-1|

The goal of this annual report for Zumtobel, a European manufacturer of lighting systems, was to convey a message of prosperity and success to its shareholders. Its cover, **(a)** a sculpture molded in plastic relief, reappears on the report's interior pages **(b,c)** as a means of demonstrating the different lighting effects that Zumtobel's products can create. Showing different lighting effects supports the publication's goal by giving shareholders a demonstration of the product's effectiveness. The unexpected surprise of actual molded front and back covers **(d)** also supports the goal by sending a message that Zumtobel is creative and innovative—attributes that are important to continued success in this market. (Annual report design by Sagmeister, Inc.)

It is important to know the psychological foundations of the members of the group (their behavior, how they think and feel and interact) before a design concept can be formed. Combining these psychological foundations with statistical information, or *demographics*, such as age, gender, ethnicity, geography, and income, forms a basis for determining what types of messages, imagery, and visual approach will appeal to an audience. (See Figure 2-2).

Consider the Venue

Venue refers to the place where a publication will be seen and read. Both aspects influence a publication's design and format, however they differ from each other in that a publication's

Figure |2-2|

YM is a lifestyle magazine for teenage girls. Like many magazines directed at this audience, the content of *YM* includes fashion features that keep readers informed about the latest trends. To connect with its audience on a more intimate level, *YM* personalized the experience for them by picking a teenage girl named "Sophie" and treating the feature as though it was a segment from her diary. The graphic treatment of the pages and their pictures connects with readers on a personal and meaningful level because they mirror their real-life experiences. (*YM* magazine design by Amy Demas)

cover may perform in one venue, while its interior pages perform in another. When a publication is first seen in the retail venue, such as a bookstore or newsstand, its cover acts as a point-of-purchase display. A book cover, for instance, must catch the attention of a potential reader and instantly communicate what the reading experience will be like. (See Figure 2-3).

The portability, ease of use, and reader friendliness of a book are also important factors in determining its format and design. Reference manuals and cookbooks are made more useful when

Figure |2-3|

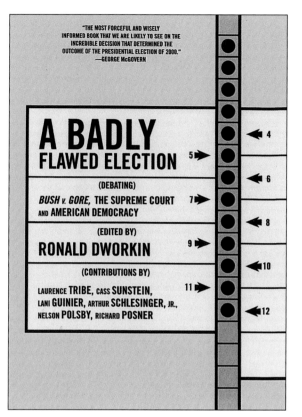

A Badly Flawed Election is about the 2000 presidential election and its controversial outcome. Because the butterfly ballot was at the core of the confusion over how to count the ballots in the pivotal state of Florida, it proved to be the perfect symbol as a visual theme for this cover design. With this graphic treatment on its cover, the book's subject matter is communicated in an instant to those who encounter it in a bookstore. (Cover design by Gary Tooth, Empire Design Studio)

they are bound in a way that allows them to be laid open on a flat surface. Books directed at preschoolers usually have lots of pictures and few words so that they will engage their audience and encourage them to try to understand what they read. (See Figure 2-4).

Do the Research

After the primary goal, audience, and venue for a publication have been determined, research follows to determine what direction the design will take. It often helps to make comparisons with similar or competitive publications as well as products or other materials with similar goals and audiences.

Research, done at the library or through the internet, can provide many opportunities for inspiration. It can help a designer make social and cultural connections, and arrive at appropriate color schemes, typeface choices, and stylistic approaches that will appeal to a targeted audience. Research can also yield sources for imagery, stylistic, social, and cultural references as well as additional information on a publication's goal and audience.

Figure |2-4|

This pocket guide measures just 6 × 4 inches. Its small size allows campers and hikers to easily fit this handy reference book in a pocket or backpack. (Book cover design courtesy of Chanticleer Press, Inc.)

Other Considerations

In the "real world," a publication's production budget and time line have a major impact on its design. Budget affects the size of a publication, (its dimensions and number of pages) as well as the number of images it includes and the color that is printed. Budget also has an impact on the degree of quality that is perceived, affecting the choice and grade of the paper that is used as well as the durability of a publication's cover and binding.

A tight deadline can also affect a publication's design. Certain types of cover and binding treatments require more lead time than others. Publications with many pages, lots of imagery, and color also require more time to produce.

Develop a Strategy

The design phase begins only when all of the preceding factors have been considered and research has been done. Concepts for an overall look or attitude usually begin to emerge as a result of going through these steps.

Unlike posters or other single-page design projects, publications are complex in that they consist of many pages contained within two covers. The pages within a publication may be similar or different, depending on the content and goal of the publication. For instance, most magazines have a table of contents, column or department pages, and a feature section. The pages in each of these sections have a distinct appearance that helps the reader differentiate one section from the next, but they are unified by a similar look or attitude that satisfies the publication's goal.

A Strategy That Inspires

As a manufacturer of fine printing papers, Gilbert Paper found it advantageous to collaborate with interior designer Holly Hunt in developing a collection of colors for its Oxford paper line, an uncoated stock known for its rich, textural finish. Hunt's color expertise and eye for current trends made her an ideal candidate for putting together a fashion-conscious, harmonious palette.

When the new color palette was selected, the paper manufacturer wanted to introduce the new Oxford line to its audience of graphic designers with a promotional brochure printed on Oxford paper. The brochure needed to attract and inspire designers as well as show how well the paper performs under various printing and production situations. Its content would focus on Hunt's approach to interior design—a philosophy based on directness, simplicity, and comfort that is manifested in contemporary furnishings that project understated elegance and sophistication.

The brochure's designer, Rick Valicenti of Thirst, developed a design strategy that echoes Hunt's design sensibility and supports the publication's goal by showcasing the paper's capability and inspiring designers on many different levels. The cover (Figure 2-5a) supports Hunt's philosophy with its elegant simplicity and the slim lines of the

(a)

(b)

(c)

(continued)

A Strategy That Inspires (cont.)

Oxford line's new logo. The logo's incorporation of an O and X along with the letter H, serves as a metaphor for the collaboration between Hunt and Oxford and is used as a unifying element throughout the brochure. It reappears on the brochure's opening pages that feature a selection of fabric swatches Hunt uses in her furnishings (Figure 2-5b). The fabric colors on these pages reappear in photographs of Hunt's furniture designs, where rich color reproduction and crisp detail demonstrate the printing capability of the Oxford paper (Figure 2-5c). Other pages incorporate intricate die cuts to reinforce the shapes formed by the logo design and show how well the paper performs under these production circumstances (Figure 2-5d). Valicenti's brochure design goes even further to make the most of the new colors by including actual paper swatches that suggest other designs and invite interactivity (Figure 2-5e). His novel and harmonious integration of design and utility help make this promotional brochure both inspirational and useful to designers who are considering using this paper for their projects.

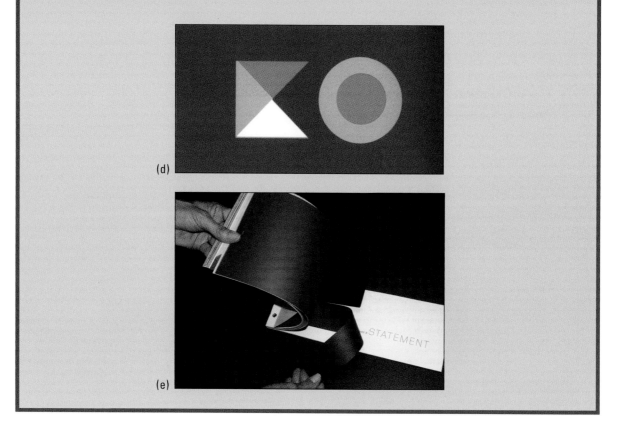

(d)

(e)

A publication designer will come up with a design strategy that projects an image or attitude that appeals to the target audience and satisfies the publication's goal. This strategy will include a color palette, typography, a plan for imagery, and an overall format or structure for the publication. A successful design strategy will also meet the project's budget and time-line constraints. The design strategy serves as a plan or blueprint for the publication.

Design Principles

If the design strategy serves as a plan or blueprint for a publication, it can be useful to think of the elements of design as structural components and the design principles as the tools. Principles help a designer determine the relationship between the parts or design elements involved and serve as rules that a designer can follow when combining these elements in a design. Within the realm of publication design, these elements and principles are combined in a *layout*. In publication design, a layout is a composed page or cover design. In any given layout, some principles will likely have a more dominant function, whereas others serve a supporting role. Before design decisions can be made, it is important to understand what each of these principles involves.

Hierarchy

Hierarchy is achieved by determining dominance or emphasizing one design element over another. In some cases, it is obvious which elements in a layout need to be most dominant, such as the photograph of a new car on the cover of a brochure that promotes it. However, often the designer determines which elements will dominate and which will be subordinate, and develops an arranged order by controlling size, placement, color, and balance of these elements. This arrangement determines the path the viewer's eye will take as it scans a layout.

Lack of clear visual hierarchy is the reason many designs fail to attract and hold a viewer's attention. It is important that one element be dominant to give the viewer's eye a *focal point*. There should also be an underlying order of emphasis for other elements in the design. There should never be a "power struggle" between design elements. (See Figure 2-6).

Balance

We strive for balance in all aspects of our lives. A diet of too many starchy foods is not balanced. If we work too hard and don't take time to relax, our lives feel out of balance. Balance is also an important component in design. When design elements are not in balance, the viewer feels uncomfortable.

Balance in a design refers to the equal distribution of visual weight in a layout. In any layout, some visual elements have more optical weight or dominance than others. It is the designer's role to arrange these visual elements so that they are in optical balance.

There are two approaches to achieving balance in a layout: symmetric and asymmetric. In a symmetrically balanced layout, identical or similar design elements are aligned in an equal way on either side of a vertical axis. Symmetrically balanced layouts tend to be more formal and static in their appearance. (See Figure 2-7).

In an asymmetrical layout, balance is achieved with an unequal arrangement of elements. Asymmetrical layouts tend to look more casual than those that are symmetrically balanced.

(a)

(b)

(c)

Figure |2-6|

In these three cover layouts, size determines which composition element is seen first and which becomes secondary. **(a)** The photograph, title, and subtitle all have equal emphasis—none is more dominant than another. **(b)** The photograph is the most dominant element and catches the eye first. **(c)** The most dominant element is the typography, the photograph is of secondary interest. (Photo by Margaret Plowdrey).

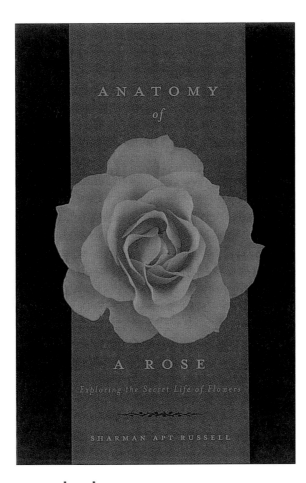

Figure |2-7|

This book cover features a symmetrical layout. If a vertical axis were drawn down the middle, the left half of the cover would mirror the right. (Cover design by Kimberly Glyder Design)

However, achieving asymmetrical balance is more difficult and complex because the visual weight of each element and their arrangement needs to be carefully considered. Balance can often be achieved by balancing positive with negative space, or form with counterform. (See Figure 2-8).

Proximity

The placement of design elements together and apart from one another is a function of proximity. Equal spacing between elements in a composition often results in a static, boring design. However, proportional variation in the placement of elements results in a kinetic tension that brings interest and excitement to a layout.

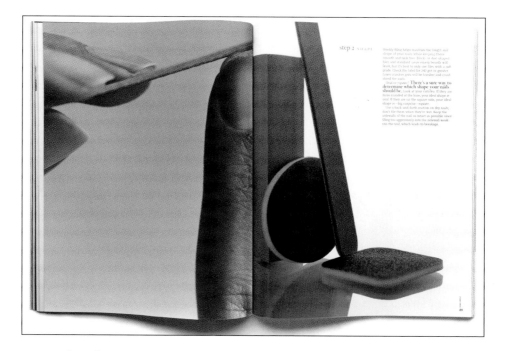

Figure |2-8|

This magazine spread demonstrates how an asymmetrical layout balances form and counterform, or positive and negative shapes. Roughly equivalent positive and negative areas offset each other within the photograph on the left, as well as the right-hand page where the imagery on the lower left is counterbalanced by the negative space in the upper right. (*Real Simple* feature layout by Robert Valentine)

The space between two or more elements affects their relationship. Visual tension results as they move together, and when they touch, hybrid shapes can form. Proximity groupings of several design elements can create patterns, a sense of rhythm or other relationships, such as ambiguity between figure and ground. Groupings where elements are layered or one element overlaps another can create the illusion of depth. (See Figure 2-9).

Rhythm, Pattern, and Texture

In music, rhythm refers to a pattern of alternating occurrences of sound and silence. Rhythm in design is similar in that it is a pattern that is created by repeating visual elements and establishing a sense of movement from one element to the next. Sound and silence are replaced with form and space.

Texture is closely related to pattern in that texture is a biproduct of repetition, but it differs from pattern in that the perception of the shapes, lines, or typographic forms that were used in its creation are overridden by the sense of texture that is achieved. (See Figure 2-10).

Figure | 2-9 |

Visual interest is created in this brochure layout by the spacial relationships that occur between the pink and black card symbols. The placement of the spade, heart, and club shapes causes hybrid shapes to occur between them, creating ambiguity between figure and ground. (Layout design by Bradbury Thompson, courtesy of Westvaco)

Texture is not a design principle or element on its own, but can enhance the quality of elements in a layout by giving them surface characteristics. Texture can imply tactile characteristics by simulating surfaces such as fur or granite. Texture can be created by digitally scanning actual objects or by using markers, pen-and-ink, paint, and pencil to create textural effects. Designers use texture to achieve richness, variety, and depth in a composition and to help differentiate figure from ground. (See Figure 2-11).

Scale

Scale is the size relationships between the various elements in a layout and can be used to control emphasis and hierarchy. A sense of perspective, or the illusion of depth, is an aspect of scale. Spatial depth can be achieved by placing large elements in the front and smaller elements in the back. Overlapping shapes can increase the illusion of spatial depth. (See Figure 2-12).

Scale is often relative to what we are accustomed to seeing and experiencing. Because we are used to thinking of an elephant as large and a fly as small, a scale reversal, where a fly is seen as large and imposing, can create visual interest and surprise by presenting the viewer with something unexpected. Using contrast of scale, where one element in a layout overpowers another, can result in intriguing relationships between design elements.

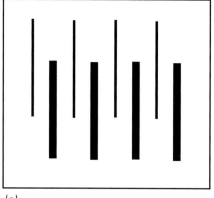

(a)

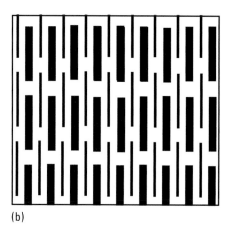

(b)

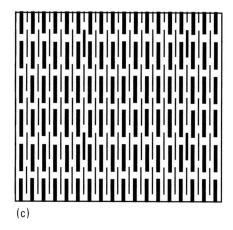

(c)

Figure | 2-10 |

Rhythm, pattern, and texture are closely related in that they are all aspects of repetition. **(a)** A sense of rhythm is established by the positioning of linear elements. When this rhythmic design is reduced and repeated as it is in example **(b)** it becomes a pattern **(c)**. As the original design is further reduced and repeated, it is perceived as texture.

Unity and Variety

Unity is achieved by choosing and organizing design elements in a way that creates a sense of wholeness and harmony. Unity can be easily achieved when all elements in a composition are the same. However, too much sameness can result in a boring composition.

Figure |2-11|

The perception of texture in this book cover design exists on several levels: The tactileness of paper is conveyed by its realistic representation as background. The designer scanned graph and lined note paper to create this effect. A sense of visual texture exists in the cross-hatching that is used to contour the horse's hind quarters and in the subtle pencil rendering of the tubular image in the upper left corner. (Cover design and illustration by John Gall, Ned Drew, Vintage Books)

Figure |2-12|

Scale is used in this magazine layout to suggest spatial depth. The photograph of the flying children on the right is large and makes them appear as though they are in the foreground. A similar photograph, on a reduced scale, is positioned in the upper left corner to give the impression that they are flying in the distance. (Magazine design by Gael Towey)

As a complementary principle, variety involves choosing and adding different elements for visual interest. Too much variety, or random use of it, can cause confusion. The most effective design solutions achieve a balance between unity and variety by arriving at a harmonious combination of design elements that are similar in subtle ways, yet varied enough to be visually stimulating. (See Figure 2-13).

Figure | 2-13 |

It was important to have a consistent graphic treatment for author Rick Moody's novels so that his fans could easily recognize his books by their distinctive look. Typography in the same style and size, and a pastel color palette helped to unify the covers. Because the covers employ an object referenced in each of Moody's books, the central image on each is unique, helping to create variety and differentiate one title from the next. (Cover designs by Paul Sahre, Office of Paul Sahre and Mario Pulice, Little, Brown and Company)

Design Elements

Design elements are the components or the parts that make up a design composition. The formal elements of design, shape, line, and color, are abstract in nature, meaning that they do not describe anything. However, they can be used to represent an object. A circular shape, for instance, can represent the moon in a composition. Designers arrange elements in a layout in support of the publication's goal and give them order using the principles described earlier in this chapter. (See Figure 2-14).

Shape

Shape is the form or outline of something. It can also be described as form or mass. In computer programs, shape is often described as a closed form or closed path. In two-dimensional design, a shape has width and length but not three-dimensional mass. A shape can be

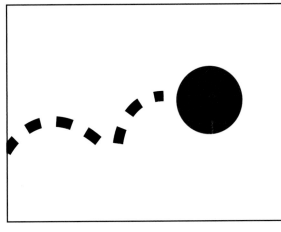

(a)

Figure | 2-14 |

These compositions are similar in that both include a red circle and linear elements. The red circle in each composition is sized and positioned the same, but is perceived differently, depending on how the linear elements are handled. **(a)** The linear element is a curved dotted line that suggests a bouncing movement, causing the circle to be perceived as a ball. **(b)** The linear element is a series of wavy lines that are reduced in scale, so they appear to recede. The viewer perceives a horizon, and the circle becomes the sun or a full moon over a body of water.

(b)

Figure |2-15|

(a) The circle is defined by a line or a stroked path. **(b)** The circle is described as a shape or filled path.

described by a line that defines its edge, or it can be defined by an edge that is clear and distinct. (See Figure 2-15).

Shapes exist as figures in or on a ground. Although they are generally considered as positive figures displacing space, the negative space, or the space around a figure, has shape as well. Harmonic relationships occur when a designer pays attention to both of these aspects. Dynamic visual activity develops when ambiguity exists between positive shapes and the negative spaces surrounding them. (See Figure 2-16).

Figure |2-16|

Interesting visual relationships develop when the viewer is not sure which shapes in a composition are foreground or background. This phenomenon, called "figure/ground ambiguity," is used in this magazine layout. It is hard to tell if the black shape containing text and the half circle above it is imposed on the white area, or if the white ground has been cut away, revealing these shapes beneath as background. (Magazine design by Florian Bachleda)

Line

A line is a path connecting two or more points. Although computer programs describe lines as paths, a line can also be a mark made by a tool that is drawn across a surface to describe a path. Lines can be straight or angular, or they can meander and curve.

The quality or look of a line is an aspect of the tool that makes it, and it can communicate a mood or attitude. For instance, a line drawn with charcoal has a soft, organic quality. One drawn with pen-and-ink is crisp and precise.

Lines can also indicate direction. Horizontal lines in a composition guide a viewer's eye from left to right. Vertical lines direct a viewer's gaze downward and upward.

Lines are often implied. Alignment of type or shaped elements in a composition can create implied linear relationships. Linear relationships can activate compositional space by helping to direct the viewer's eye. (See Figure 2-17).

Color

Like texture, color enhances the elements in a layout by helping to activate shapes and space and by creating emphasis and supporting hierarchy. Designers who understand how to use color effectively can use it to create a sense of spacial depth and emphasis, and guide a viewer's eye through a layout. Color can also be a powerful means of communicating emotion and can be a useful unifying device in publication design. You'll learn more about how to use color to support a design or layout in Chapter Three: Using Color Effectively.

Figure |2-17|

In this magazine layout, an indirect linear relationship exists between the illustration on the left and the feature title on the right. The gaze of the illustration's subjects and the diagonal lines created by the black and white background shapes all help direct the viewer's eye from left to right. (*Bloomberg Markets* layout design by Carol Macrini, Tamar Davis; illustration by Joe Ciardiello)

In this chapter, a discussion of color theory is limited to a brief glossary of color-related terms to refamiliarize you with basic color attributes and terminology. Because a thorough understanding of color theory is an important part of any designer's education, study other resources that will give you a more complete understanding of color if you have not had a formal introduction to color theory.

Hue—The essence or name of a color (e.g., red, blue, green). Value—The darkness or lightness of a color. Colors with black added are called *shades*. *Tints* are colors to which white has been added. Light colors such as yellow are called *high-key*. Dark color such as violet are called *low-key*. Saturation—The brightness or

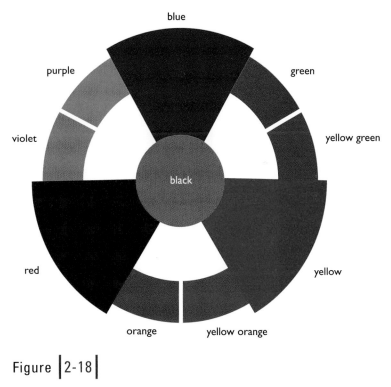

Figure |2-18|

Additional terms to help you in your understanding of color involve the positioning of colors on the color wheel. The color wheel shown here represents the **subtractive** color system, which is based on mixing pigments.

dullness of a color. When black, white, gray, or a color's complement is added, a color becomes less saturated. (Also called *chroma* or *intensity*) (See Figure 2-18).

Primary hues—Red, yellow, and blue.

Secondary hues—Green, orange, and purple.

Complements—Colors that are directly opposite one another on the color wheel (e.g., red and green).

Type

The principles that apply to the other formal design elements also apply to type. Type is a component in page and cover layout that is controlled and arranged with other elements in support of the publication's communication goal. However, type plays a dual role in that typographic forms also contain verbal meaning. It is as important for typography to effectively communicate a verbal message as well as function well in a design composition.

Text, whether it is set in a rectangular format or configured to form a shape, functions as a design element in a layout. The amount of emphasis that a text-filled shape has in a layout is largely a result of its scale and the size, weight, and style of the typeface that is used. (See Figure 2-19).

Figure |2-19|

The circular shape of the text in this magazine layout is a departure from the traditional rectangular column format. In addition to adding an element of the unexpected, the organic quality of this configuration is visually more compatible with the expanse of water in the background. (*Vanity Fair* layout design by David Harris, Julie Weiss and Chris Israel, photograph by Annie Leibovitz)

Figure |2-20|

The large and imposing letterforms in the word "lights" create interesting positive and negative shapes in this magazine layout. The photographer's credit, which is turned on its side, adds a linear element to the layout that helps to balance the text below it. (*Texas Monthly* magazine design by Scott Dadich, photograph by Dan Winters)

Typographic forms can be used to create shapes and harmonious figure/ground relationships in a layout. Many typographic forms, by themselves, are beautiful and appealing to the eye. The positive and negative shapes that occur between arrangements of letterforms and numerals can also yield many intriguing visual possibilities. Typographic forms can also be layered to create spatial depth.

Type also performs as a linear element in a composition, helping to guide a viewer's eye. Typographic forms can be arranged in a way that implies linear direction, or they can be configured into a straight line or a curve to direct a viewer's gaze. (See Figure 2-20).

Just as a block of text serves as shape in a composition, the quality of the text within that block can lend texture to that shape. Textural effects or patterns can also be created by repeating typographic forms. (See Figure 2-21).

Type can also be used to support attitude or mood. You'll learn more about how to use type in this manner as well as other rules and conventions for using type in Chapter Four, "Understanding Type."

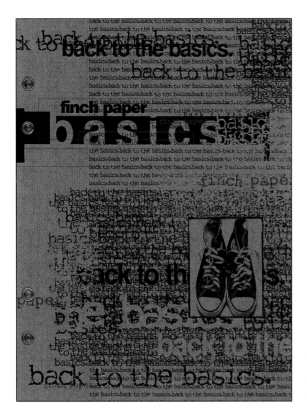

Figure |2-21|

The typographic texture on the cover of this promotional brochure was created by layering type in a variety of sizes and weights. (Design by Robert DeLuke, Finch Paper)

Imagery

Although not a formal element of design, imagery can function as a design element in page and page layout. Imagery can take the form of a photograph or illustration. It can be framed in a rectangular or circular format, or it can function as an outlined shape (without background) in a layout. A designer may be given imagery to work with, be given the task of supplying an image, or be given the option to decide whether or not imagery is important to meeting the design objective. You will learn more about working with imagery in Chapter Five, "Page Layout," and Chapter Six: "Imagery."

Organizing Content

Earlier in this chapter you learned about the importance of emphasis and hierarchy in page and cover layout. Understanding which design element should receive the most emphasis and which ones should play a supportive role is the first step in determining an arrangement. From there, the next step involves developing an underlying structure for organizing this arrangement.

Proportional Systems and Grids

Over the years, architects, artists and designers have used proportional systems or *grids* to give organization and structure to visual elements in a design. A grid supplies an underlying structure or a transparent framework for determining where to align graphic elements, imagery,

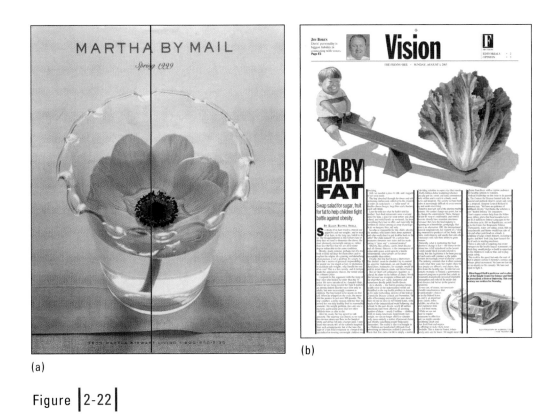

(a)

(b)

Figure │2-22│

(a) The symmetric layout of the catalog cover design uses a single line running through its center as a method of alignment. The title and cover image are centered on this grid line. (Catalog cover design by Martha Stewart Omnimedia) **(b)** A more complex grid system wherein headlines, text, and imagery are aligned to a four-column grid. (*Fresno Bee* page layout and illustration by Gabe Utasi)

and text in a layout. A grid can be as simple as an invisible guide line running through a layout, or it can be a more complex system. (See Figure 2-22).

Proportion is how a page is segmented. Proportional systems determine how a grid will be developed. Historically, optically pleasing arrangements have been based on proportional relationships found in nature. The *golden mean*, for instance, is based on a harmonic arrangement that has been found in plants and other life forms. It even exists in the human body. If you measure your body from foot to navel, then from navel to the top of your head, you will find the ratio between these measurements is 1 to 1.6. This mathematic ratio can be expressed in a proportionately sectioned rectangle as shown in Figure 2-23a. The Ancient Greeks understood this ratio and applied it to the proportions of the Parthenon. Designers often apply this principle today to serve as a guide for organizing text and visuals in a layout. (See Figure 2-23b).

Other alignment principles commonly applied to page layouts are based on similar proportional relationships that have been proven, over time, to be optically pleasing. The *line of golden proportion*, for instance, is based on dividing a page into eighths and placing a design element or single line of text at a point so it is at three-eighths from the top of a page. (See Figure 2-24).

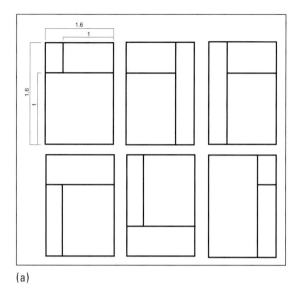

(a)

(b)

Figure |2-23|

(a) Several grid variations wherein a rectangle is broken down into three segments based on the golden mean. **(b)** A brochure cover based on the golden mean. (Brochure design by Bernhardt Fudyma)

(b)

(a)

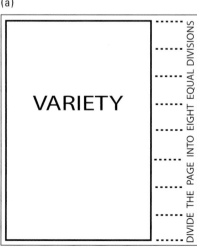

VARIETY

DIVIDE THE PAGE INTO EIGHT EQUAL DIVISIONS

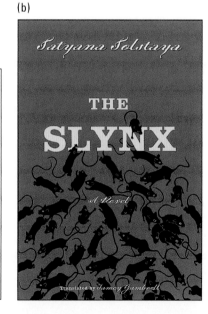

Figure |2-24|

(a) The line of golden proportion is based on placing the most dominant design element at a point that is three-eighths from the top of a page. **(b)** The line of golden proportion principle applied to a book cover. (Book cover design by Michaela Sullivan, Houghton Mifflin Company; illustration by Luba Lukova)

It is the designer's job to develop a grid that will support the publication's content and visuals. Complex grids comprised of a series of horizontal and vertical lines provide a system for determining mathematically precise, modular units of text, visuals, and other graphic elements that comprise a page layout. In Chapter Five, "Page Layout," you will learn more about grids and how to use them in support of a design.

Directing Eye Movement

After a grid or method of alignment has been decided upon, hierarchy and emphasis play an important role in guiding a viewer's eye through a layout. The designer determines which element is most important and will be the first to catch a viewer's attention. From there, design elements with secondary importance (followed by those with even less importance) lead the viewer's gaze through a layout so that the eye moves in a way that takes in all of the visual content.

The positioning of elements on a page, their size, color, and visual weight, as well as their relationship to one another all affect hierarchy. Here are some guidelines to keep in mind when determining what elements will be seen first and which will play a subordinate role:

- Position—In Western culture, we tend to read from left to right and from top to bottom. As a result, elements in a layout that are positioned at the top and to the left are likely to be seen first.
- Scale—Large items in a layout tend to draw the eye. The smallest elements tend to be seen last.
- Contrast—Areas of high contrast tend to dominate in a layout, whereas areas of low contrast tend to recede.
- Implied direction—Linear elements, edges, elements in a line, or even an image such as a face in profile, can direct a viewer's gaze. (See Figure 2-25).

SUMMARY

Publications exist to inform, persuade, sell, or entertain. Before designing a publication, it is important to do research in order to fully understand a publication's goal and its audience. The publication's budget and its venue (where it will be sold and read) are also important factors in developing a design strategy.

Once a strategy has been determined, basic principles and elements guide the design process. The elements of design are the visual components in a page or cover layout. The principles are the rules that help designers determine the relationship between the design elements in a layout.

The basic principles of design are:

- Hierarchy—determining what will be most dominant
- Balance—equal distribution of visual weight
- Proximity—determining spatial relationships between design elements

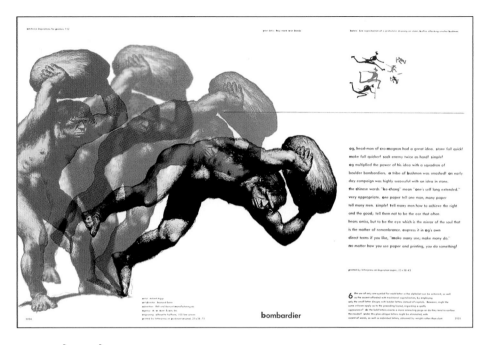

Figure |2-25|

Several principles work to direct the viewer's gaze through this layout. The design starts with the premise that the viewer's eye will naturally gravitate from left to right (the way we are accustomed to reading in Western culture) and takes advantage of dominance of scale by placing the largest element, the caveman, to the left. The positioning of the caveman, so he is leaning toward the right, and repeating this image supports the left to right movement. The darkest and most dominant of these multiple images is the caveman printed in black, who stands out in most contrast against the white background. From there, the viewer is directed to the smallest design element in this layout—the column of text to the far right. (Layout design by Bradbury Thompson, courtesy of Westvaco)

- Rhythm, pattern, and texture—repetition of design elements
- Scale—relative size of design elements
- Unity and variety—what will be the same and what will be different

The basic elements of design are:

- Shape
- Line
- Color
- Type
- Imagery

Content in a publication is organized using harmonious proportion systems called grids. Grids provide structure and a means of determining alignment for graphic elements, imagery, and text in a layout.

in review

1. Name four goal categories.

2. What are demographics and what do they mean in publication design?

3. What is venue and why is this important to publication design?

4. How does a publication's design support its communication goal?

5. What is hierarchy and why is it important in a layout?

6. What is the difference between symmetric and an asymmetric balance?

7. What is proximity?

8. What are the differences between rhythm, pattern, and texture?

9. How does scale work to create the illusion of space?

10. Why are unity and variety important in creating a harmonic design?

11. What is figure ground ambiguity?

12. What aspects of type allow it to work in a layout as a design element?

13. What is a grid and how does it function in a layout?

14. What is the golden mean?

projects

Project Title Typography Book Cover

Project Brief Develop a book cover for the following imaginary title: Typography and Great Design. Use an $8\frac{1}{2} \times 10$-inch format and limit your design to black and white and shades of gray. Your design should be limited to just the title and include no imagery and should place the most emphasis on the word "Typography." Come up with two typographic design solutions that demonstrate each of the following:

Type as Shape
Type as Line

Apply the basic principles and elements of design that were discussed in this chapter to come up with pleasing compositions for both of these cover solutions.

Objectives

Appreciate how type can work as shape and line in a composition. Apply principles such as scale, contrast and proximity, to achieve typographical hierarchy in layout.

Project Title Textured Cover

Project Brief Using the "Type as Shape" example that you created in the above exercise, create a second version of this cover design that adds texture to the original design. Maintain the same 8 ½ × 10-inch format and limit your palette to black, white, and gray. Use texture in the same way you would use gray in your composition, as a way of adding tone and variation to a black-and-white composition.

Objectives

Understand how texture can add visual interest and tone to a design composition.

Project Title Magazine Cover Scavenger Hunt

Project Brief Find covers from magazines that are directed to each of the following audiences:

Youthful
Primarily Male
Primarily Female

Answer the following questions for each of these covers:

1. What or who is featured on the cover and how does this subject connect with the magazine's intended audience?

2. Compare and contrast the mastheads or logos for each of these magazines. How are they different from each other?

3. Identify other features on these covers, such as type styles, colors, and other graphic elements that you believe help each of these magazines connect with their intended audience.

Objectives

Appreciate how type, color and other design attributes can project a sensibility that attracts a specific audience.

notes

SQA Catalog

| using color effectively |

SQA

3

objectives

Learn how color can help establish a mood for a publication, cover or article design.

Explore various color combinations and understand why certain colors work well together, and others do not.

Understand how color can help create hierarchy and control space in a layout.

See how color can work as a unifying element in a publication.

Explore how color is perceived and used in the digital realm and in print.

Learn about color systems and how they are applied in publication design and production.

introduction

The importance of color in visual communication cannot be overstated. Its emotive power is a significant factor in publication, as well as other types of design. Certain colors and color combinations can immediately stir feelings in a viewer or help them identify with a social or cultural theme.

Color can also enhance a publication's design by activating shapes and text as well as other graphic elements in a layout. Publication designers who know how to work with color effectively use it, in concert with other design principles, to control hierarchy and emphasis in a layout. Color can also be used as a unifying element on a cover or a page, as well as throughout an entire publication.

This chapter explores the importance of color and how it can be used most effectively to support a publication's communication goal and design.

Color and Mood

Color is a language that is universally understood. We can predict, with some degree of certainty, that people will respond in a consistent way when they see a certain color or color combination. Although some colors have universal meaning, other colors and color combinations have social or cultural connotation. It is important to understand these differences and to select colors for a publication's design that will connect with an audience or communicate a mood that is in support of a publication's communication goal.

Cross-Cultural Color

Human beings make psychological connections between the colors they see and associate them with elements that are common to all humans regardless of age, gender, or nationality. These psychological connections date back to our primitive roots. For instance blue, because it is associated with water and the sky, is perceived as calming and constant. We feel these emotions because they are connected with our knowledge that the sky and the oceans will always be there.

Much of a viewer's reaction to color is subliminal and has its foundations in these primitive associations. Corporate decision makers, as well as designers, are aware of these psychological connections and consider them when making decisions about color. Because blue is inter-

Figure |3-1|

Because blue is associated with stability, corporations such as IBM often choose this color to instill a sense of trust in consumers. (Package design courtesey of Libby Perzyk Kathman)

preted as constant and reliable, it is no accident that banks and other institutions wanting to instill a feeling of stability and security in consumers, frequently choose blue as their corporate color. (See Figure 3-1).

In addition to its psychological impact, color can have a significant physiologic effect on viewers. Scientific experiments have shown that long-term exposure to an intense and fully saturated version of the color red can increase blood pressure and respiration, as well as cause a faster heartbeat. Our reaction to red stems from primitive associations with blood and fire. Because red excites us and catches our attention, it is used for stop signs and often appears in other applications wherein somebody is trying to catch our attention. (See Figure 3-2).

Color and its Cultural Significance

Certain colors and color combinations can also have social or cultural meaning. A familiar example is the combination of red, white, and blue. Because they are the colors of the American flag, red, white, and blue are typically used in the design of literature with the goal of generating patriotic feelings among American

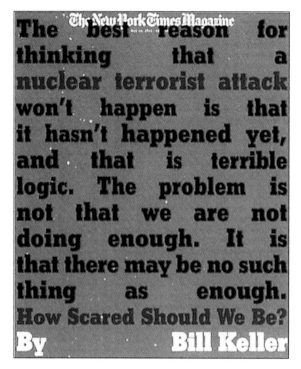

Figure |3-2|

A sense of urgency is communicated in this cover design for *The New York Times Magazine* by drawing the viewer's attention to key phrases printed in bright red. (Cover design by Janet Froelich and Lisa Naftolin)

Color Psychology

The following are common associations between colors and their psychological implications in Western culture:

     Blue: Calming, honesty, cool, reliable, sad

     Red: Stimulating, exciting, dangerous, aggressive, sexy

     Yellow: Sunlight, citrus, imaginative, cheerful, cowardly

     Purple: Regal, majestic, creative, futuristic

     Orange: Hot, active, tangy, childlike, gregarious

     Green: Nature, growth, financial wealth

     White: Pure, innocent, clean

     Black: Elegant, mysterious, ominous, sober, sophisticated

     Brown: Earthy, organic, rich, flavorful

citizens. Color is often used this way to make a direct connection with a specific audience or demographic group. Although people of other cultures may also associate these colors with the American flag, the reaction of patriotism is distinct among Americans. Viewers in other countries may not react in the same way because they are not likely to make an emotional connection with these colors the way Americans do. (See Figure 3-3).

Other colors and color combinations can have different meaning to different cultures. In America, green is connected with financial wealth because it is the color of American currency. Because of this association, green is often featured prominently in the design of literature promoting financial seminars, loan programs, and other organizations and events focused on money management and financial wealth. (See Figure 3-4). However, in Indian culture, green is associated with spiritual harmony—quite the opposite of its meaning to Americans. As communication between cultures increases and because each culture has its own unique heritage of color symbolism, it is important to do research to determine the perception of color in a given culture before designing a piece specific to that culture.

In Western culture, certain colors and color combinations are perceived as gender- or age-specific. Blue, for instance, is considered to be a masculine color. (See Figure 3-5). Pink is associated with a

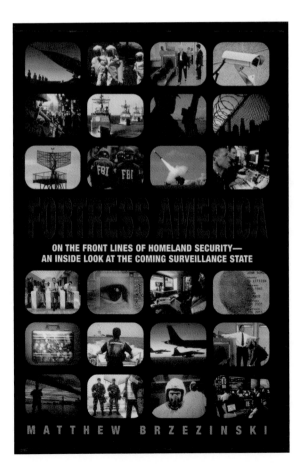

Figure |3-3|

This book addressing American security is not about patriotism or American politics; however, incorporating red, white, and blue into its color scheme is likely to attract American citizens with strong patriotic feelings. Note that the predominant use of red in the title also communicates a sense of alert.

Figure | 3-4 |

Green, because of its association with money and finance, plays a prominent role in H&R Block's literature and corporate identity. (H&R Block identity design by Landor Associates).

youthful, feminine look. We associate the pastel primaries of pink, blue, and yellow with infants. These colors often appear in garments and other products manufactured for this age group. Research has shown that toddlers and preschoolers are drawn to bright, highly saturated colors, which is the reason that books and products directed at this age group are dominated by a palette of bright primary and secondary colors.

Color can be regional or associated with regional culture. In fact, many of the cultural color connections we make are derived from objects specific to that culture. For instance, we associate a palette of turquoise, terra cotta, and tan with Native American culture

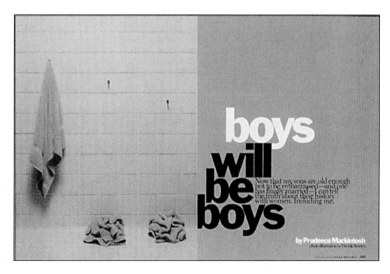

Figure | 3-5 |

Because of its association with masculinity, blue is used predominantly in this article in *Texas Monthly* magazine that focuses on the behavior of men and boys. (Design by Scott Dadich; photography by Fredrik Broden)

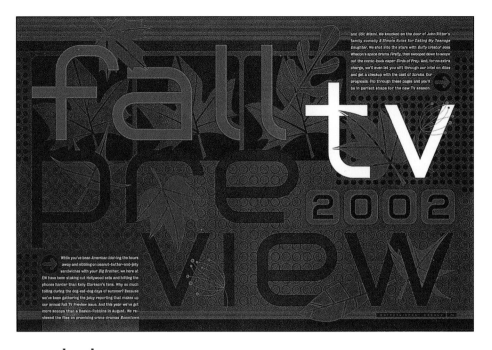

Figure |3-6|

The colors used in this magazine article for *Entertainment Weekly* reinforce its autumn theme. (Design by Geraldine Hessler and Jennifer Procopio)

and the American Southwest because they correspond with objects associated with that culture: turquoise beads, terra cotta pottery, and tan leather.

Color can communicate a range of attitudes through symbolic associations. It can be used to evoke memories of a bygone era, by mimicking the look of aged paper. Coloring a photograph with a sepia-toned tint, for instance, immediately puts that image into the context of the past. Color can be seasonal, as well. We associate shades of blue with winter and snow, and warm hues of rust, orange and yellow, the colors of autumn leaves. (See Figure 3-6).

Establishing a Harmonious Palette

Because color has such strong emotional significance, it is important to start a design concept by selecting a color or color combination that supports a publication's communication goal. Sometimes the choice is obvious, such as the book about national security with its palette of red, white, and blue that is discussed earlier.

Monochromatic Color

Pulling together a color palette for a publication should begin with the selection of a dominant color that supports the mood or attitude that needs to be expressed. In fact, a color palette for a design may consist of variations of a single color or hue. An image, composition, or layout that is limited to variations of a single color is called *monochromatic*. A monochromatic color scheme is one that is limited to tints and shades (or different values) of a single color or hue. (See Figure 3-7).

Although a monochromatic color scheme may do a good job of supporting a design's communication goal, there are times when a combination of colors may be more effective. A variety of hues can add visual interest or nuance to a publication's design and may do a better job of supporting its communication goal. When combining colors, it helps to understand why certain colors work together harmoniously and others do not.

Combinations Based on Color Complements

Color complements are colors that are opposite from each other on the color wheel. Examples of color complements are (1) violet and yellow, (2) orange and blue, and (3) red and green. When paired, fully saturated complementary colors tend to make colors appear more intense than each color would appear on its own. Paired complements, when they are next to one another, also seem to vibrate at the edges—especially when their values are equivalent, such as combining red with green or orange with blue. This type of combination can be intense and should be considered only when a brash, surprising effect is desired. However, combining

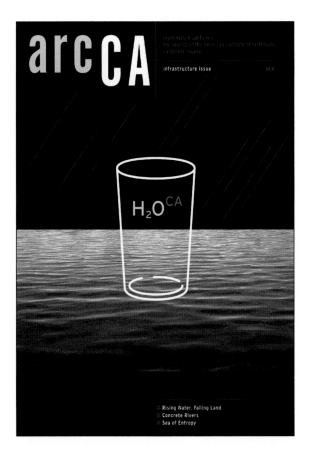

Figure |3-7|

This magazine cover uses a monochromatic color scheme based on a blue-green palette to support the focus of its contents: the importance of water and infrastructure in architecture. (Design by Aufuldish & Warinner)

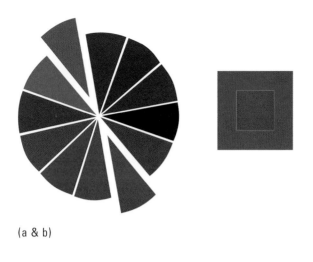

(a & b)

Figure |3-8|

(a) The color complements of blue and orange are close in value and tend to clash when they are used together in full saturation. **(b)** In this catalog cover design for Herman Miller **(c)**, the same colors work together harmoniously when they are muted by varying their value and saturation. (Catalog design by Brian Edlefson)

(c)

complementary colors that have been muted by changing their value or saturation, can result in a harmonious palette. (See Figure 3-8).

A harmonious palette can also be achieved by combining colors that are split complements. Split complements are the two colors that are in closest proximity to a color's complement. Choosing a palette of split-complements and experimenting with the value and intensity of these colors can yield a range of harmonious combinations. (See Figure 3-9).

Analogous Color Combinations

Analogous colors are neighbors on the color wheel. An analogous color combination is one that combines any three colors on the color wheel, including their tints and shades. Examples of analogous combinations are (1) blue, violet, and purple or (2) yellow, orange, and red. Combinations of these colors are guaranteed to work together. Interesting results can be achieved when changing the value or saturation of colors in an analogous palette. (See Figure 3-10).

Color Schemes Based on Triads

Combinations of colors that form triads on the color wheel can also yield harmonious results. Triads occur when hues in a color scheme are equidistant from one another on the color wheel. (See Figure 3-11).

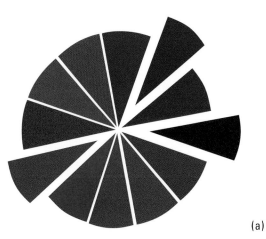

(a)

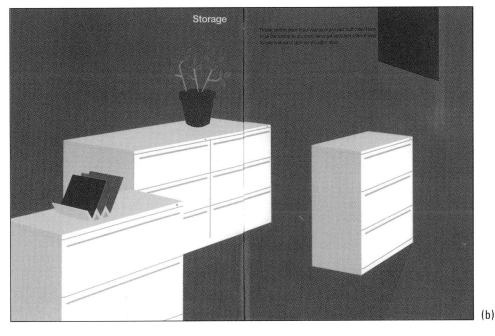

Storage

(b)

Figure |3-9|

The interior of the Herman Miller catalog **(b)** features pages that use a color palette based on split complements **(a)**. In this spread, yellow-green and the colors on either side of its complement (purple-red) are the predominant colors in the layout.

A triad also exists between the primary hues of red, blue, and yellow and between the secondary colors (those that occur when primaries are mixed) of green, orange, and violet. The elementary nature of these colors makes them a natural for children's products and books, particularly those directed at preschoolers. (See Figure 3-12).

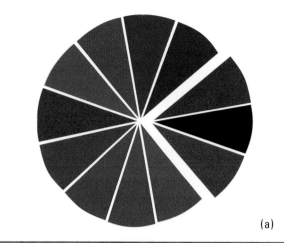

(a)

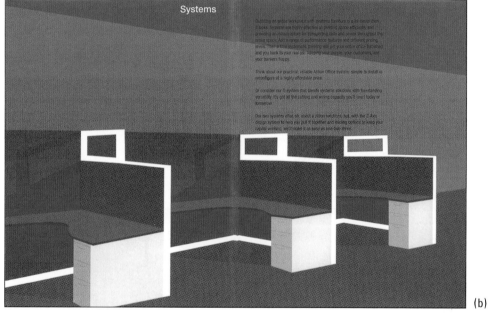

Systems

(b)

Figure |3-10|

Other pages within the Herman Miller catalog are based on an analogous color palette **(a)**. This spread **(b)** features an analogous palette of red-orange, red, and purple-red colors that are neighbors on the color wheel.

Using Color to Control Space

You learned in Chapter Two that color can support emphasis and hierarchy in design by activating type, shapes, and other design elements in a layout. Elements tend to assume a position of hierarchy in a layout because some colors have a tendency to advance or come forward, whereas others tend to fall back or recede.

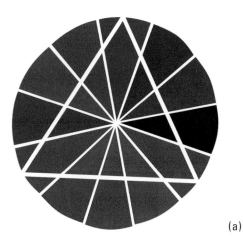

(a)

You'll still have your office furniture specified and ordered by lunch.

(b)

Figure |3-11|

The triad combination of orange, blue-green, and violet forms the basis for this harmonious palette.

Some basic rules can be applied when considering which elements will have emphasis and hierarchy in a layout. The following are attributes that should be taken into consideration when determining how color can be used to control space:

Colors That Advance

Warm colors such as red, orange, and yellow

High-saturation colors

Colors that are light in value such as yellow, pink, or beige

(a)

(b)

Figure |3-12|

Primary and secondary color triads provide an elementary palette for this children's book for early readers. (Design and illustration by Lois Ehlert, Ehlert Studio)

Colors That Recede

Cool colors such as violet, blue, and blue-green

Low-saturation colors (neutrals, brown)

Colors that are dark in value such as violet, purple, or brown

In addition, design elements that are colored so that they are in high contrast with surrounding elements tend to advance more than those that are closest in hue and value to their surrounding colors. Designers who understand how to use this principle, as well as the attributes cited above, can control what a viewer sees first and last, as well as what direction a viewer's eye will take as it loops around a layout. (See Figure 3-13).

Color as a Unifying Element

Earlier in this chapter you learned how to select colors that will work together harmoniously, and how color can be used to lead a viewer through a layout. In addition to applying these color principles to their designs, experienced designers understand that using too much color on a two-dimensional plane can be distracting. Colors begin to compete with one another, causing the viewer to become confused about where to look first and what is of secondary importance. Most designers limit their color selection to no more than three dominant hues, varying the value and saturation of these colors for variety and richness. These principles work effectively when guiding a reader's eye through a cover (See Figure 3-14), a single page, or a *spread* (left and right pages viewed together).

This theory can also be applied to an entire publication. It is as important to use just as much restraint when using color throughout a publication as you would when working with it on a single page. Experienced designers often choose a harmonious

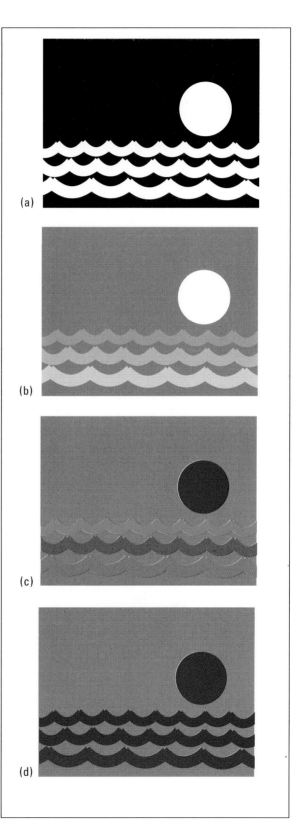

(a)

(b)

(c)

(d)

Figure | 3-13 |

(a) The wavy lines in this black-and-white perspective study appear to go back in space because their size decreases as they are repeated from bottom to top. **(b)** In this monochromatic version of the same study, the sense of depth is heightened by the change in value of each line. In this case, high-key values, or those that are lightest, tend to come forward or have most prominence, especially if they are in high contrast with their background. **(c)** When the value of the colors is equivalent, warm colors tend to advance, whereas cool colors recede. In this study, depth is achieved by assigning the warmest color (orange) to the wavy line that appears to be in the foreground. The coolest color (violet) is used for the line that appears furthest back. Green is a color that is neither warm nor cool and is used for the middle line. **(d)** This study shows how high-saturation hues come forward while those that have been toned down by adding gray tend to recede.

Figure |3-14|

This cover design for *@ Issue* magazine uses a palette that is primarily comprised of three hues: olive green, red, and violet. Pink, a lighter version of red, adds variety and richness to the palette. (Design by Kit Hinrichs, Pentagram)

palette and use it throughout a publication. Repeated use of the same color or color combination throughout a publication can act as unifying device, giving cohesiveness to a publication that might otherwise appear disjointed. (See Figure 3-15).

Color and Graphic Production

The color wheel that is initially presented in Chapter Two and that is used to demonstrate color harmonies earlier in this chapter is the color model with which you are probably most familiar. It is based on mixing the color primaries of blue, red, and yellow and was first developed by Johann Wolfgang von Goethe in the early part of the nineteenth century. Goethe developed this color wheel on the theory that a full spectrum of colors can be achieved when the three primaries are mixed with black and white. Von Goethe's color wheel is helpful when developing an understanding of color relationships, but the theory on which it is based does not apply to the way color is mixed when it is produced on the computer or on press when a publication is printed.

Perception of Color as Light

The concept of mixing color pigments on which von Goethe's color wheel is based is called *subtractive color*. The *subtractive color system* is based on perceiving color as light reflected off a surface. When we view a red stop sign, we are perceiving red as an aspect of reflected light.

Color is perceived quite differently when we view it on a computer or television screen as a consequence of projected light. Color, when it is viewed as projected light, is called *additive color*. The *additive color system* is based on the primary colors of red, green, and blue. When mixed in varying amounts, these primaries create the full spectrum of color. When equal amounts of all three colors are mixed, they produce white. The opposite of this principle can be demonstrated by directing a beam of light through a prism, where it is broken down into a full spectrum of hues. The industry uses RGB as an acronym

Figure |3-15|

The interior pages of *@ Issue* use red as a unifying element. On the table of contents **(a)**, red is used for the visuals that appear with each article listing and on the page numbers. Red appears again on a feature article to punctuate text on an opening spread. **(b)** Red is used throughout the magazine to add variety and visual interest to text. **(c)** On this spread, it appears on captions. (Design by Kit Hinrichs, Pentagram)

(a)

(b)

(c)

Figure |3-15|

Continued from page 65.

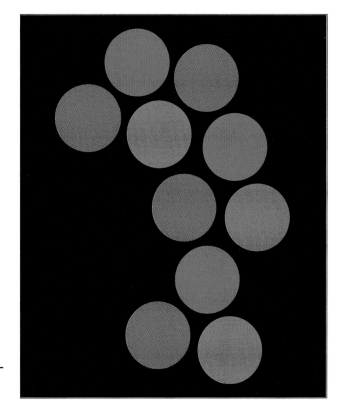

Figure |3-16|

Computer monitors and television screens display color as
distinct patterns of red, green, and blue dots or pixels.

for the additive color system. This term is used widely in computer software and other aspects
of the graphic arts industry to differentiate color viewed on a computer screen from color that
is printed. (See Figure 3-16).

Four Color Process

Because we view printed color as an aspect of perceiving color as light reflected off a surface,
it may seem logical to assume that mixing inks on paper is similar to the mixing of color pigments that serve as the basis for von Goethe's color wheel. Actually, the ability to print what
appears to be a full range of colors, as in reproducing a color photograph or other continuous
tone color image, is based on the principles of the additive color system. When mixed, the
additive primaries of red, green, and blue produce cyan, magenta, and yellow. When printed,
the blend of these secondary colors creates a range of hues. The addition of black provides a
means of adding value to these colors, allowing for a full range of color reproduction. These
four colors—cyan, magenta, yellow, and black—form the basis of the *four-color system*, also
known as *four-color process*. The abbreviation for these colors, *CMYK* (K stands for black or
key), is widely used in the graphic arts industry and related software as a means of designating four-color process or *process color*. (See Figure 3-17).

Although these four colors appear to be blended when they are viewed on a printed image, they
are not produced as a result of mixing inks. Full-color reproduction is actually achieved on press

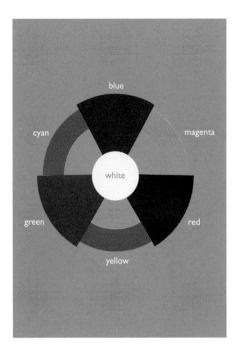

Figure |3-17|

Four-color process printing involves the mixing of cyan, magenta, and yellow, the additive secondary colors that are produced from combining the additive primaries of red, green, and blue.

by reproducing color as a series of tiny printed dots. Four-color process inks are transparent. When viewed by the naked eye, these dots overlap and blend together. Digital or reflective art (or photography) is prepared by breaking down or separating it into cyan, magenta, yellow, and black. The separation process filters these four colors and converts each to a dot pattern that is then transferred onto paper or another substrate in the printing process. (See Figure 3-18).

Match Color Systems

There are times when four-color process may not be the best means of producing printed color. For instance, four-color process can often be more expensive than a limited budget will allow. Process color also does not guarantee an exact match when printing solid areas of color. If it is important to get predictable results when printing a solid color, or if it is necessary to limit the colors printed to fewer

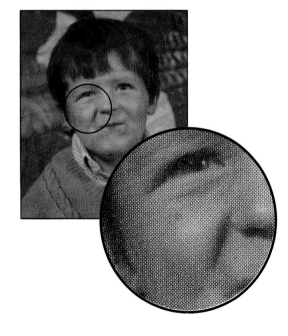

Figure |3-18|

Magnifying a printed color image shows how individual dots of cyan, magenta, yellow, and black combine to produce a range of colors.

than four colors, color is matched to an ink formula. These ink formulas are printed on color swatches that are bound into books that are widely used by designers and the graphic arts industry as a means of achieving guaranteed color on press. Designers select a color from these books and specify it by its accompanying number. The number for each color corresponds to an ink formula and serves as a code that is transferred to digital and commercial printers. The color numbering system that is the worldwide industry standard is the PANTONE MATCHING SYSTEM®, often referred to by the initials PMS. (See Figure 3-19).

In addition to PANTONE®, other match color systems include TRUMATCH®, TOYO®, and FOCALTONE®. These other systems work the same as PANTONE® and are generally available as color-specifying options on most graphic arts computer programs.

When working on the computer, designers typically select colors based on whether they are working with four-color process, PANTONE®, or another match color system. In the commercial realm, publication designers know, or make a decision before they begin designing, whether or not their design will be printed in four-color process or match colors. Occasionally, publications are printed with a combination of four-color process inks plus one or two match colors.

Experienced designers respect the inherent differences that exist between the various color systems. They also understand that color, when viewed on the computer screen, will not be an exact match to printed color, and that ink formulations produce a wider range of more brilliant colors than four-color process.

SUMMARY

Color can play an important role in achieving a publication's goal by supporting a mood or attitude. Some colors have unilateral meaning, based on primitive associations with the elements. Other colors and color combinations are attached to objects within a cultural context. The emotional reaction a viewer has to a color or color combination can sometimes depend on the meaning that color has within that individual's culture. Designers often choose a color palette for a publication by determining what color or color combination will support the publication's mood. Choosing a color palette where one hue is used is called a monochromatic color scheme.

When combining colors, the color wheel can serve as a guide for determining which combinations will work together harmoniously. Analogous colors, those that are neighbors on the color wheel, will always work together in a harmonious way. Combinations of colors that are based on split complements, a color and those colors that are adjacent to its complement, also work well together. Other harmonious

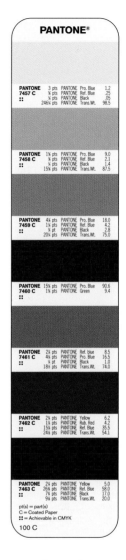

Figure | 3-19 |

This page from a PANTONE® swatch book shows variations of blue and the ink formula for each. Designers use the number that appears below each color swatch to specify that ink color. Swatch books are divided into coated and uncoated sections. In this case, the letter C after each number represents the way the color looks on coated paper.

color combinations are those based on triads, or three hues that are equidistant from each other on the color wheel.

Color can support hierarchy in a design by giving dominance to elements in a layout. High-key, warm, and highly saturated colors tend to come forward or assume most dominance, whereas low-key, cool, and more neutral colors tend to recede.

Color systems play an important role in understanding how color is perceived on a computer screen versus how it appears when it is printed. When color is seen on a computer as an aspect of projected light, it is called additive color. The additive color system is based on the additive primaries of red, blue, and green.

A range of printed colors can be achieved through four-color process, the result of combining cyan, magenta, and yellow, the additive secondary colors, with black. The four-color process system is different from match systems, which involve selecting ink colors from a swatch book.

in review

1. Name a color that has cross-cultural meaning.

2. What connotations does the color green have in American culture?

3. What are color complements? Name two colors that are color complements.

4. What is an analogous color combination? Name three colors that are analogous.

5. What are split complements? Name three colors that make a split complement palette.

6. Name three attributes of a color that are likely to make it more dominant in a design composition.

7. Why is it important to limit color in a publication's design to a selection of one to three dominant hues?

8. What is additive color? Name the three primary hues that comprise the additive color system.

9. What is subtractive color?

10. Name the four colors that comprise four-color process.

11. What is the difference between printing four-color process and printing color with a color match system? When would you specify color from a match system?

projects

Project Title   Mood/Color Scavenger Hunt

Project Brief   Find an article, book, or other published material that uses color to communicate a mood. Write an analysis that describes the colors and the mood that is being conveyed. In your analysis, consider and describe whether the color and its associated mood are cultural or cross-cultural, age-specific, seasonally related, or other.

Objectives

Recognize how color is used to communicate a feeling or attitude.

Learn how other design professionals use color in support of a mood.

Project Title Harmonious Palette Scavenger Hunt

Project Brief Find an article, book, or other published material that demonstrates each of the following color schemes:

- A monochromatic palette
- An analogous palette
- Split complements
- Color triad

Objectives

Recognize how color can be combined harmoniously.

Understand the differences between analogous, complementary, and triadic color palettes.

Learn how other design professionals combine colors harmoniously.

Project Title Color Hierarchy Compositions

Project Brief Using an 8 × 8-inch format, create a design comprised of the following: a circle, a square, and a straight or curved line. Start with a gray background and create a composition using black, white, and gray that gives equal emphasis to all three elements. You can use colored paints, a computer, or Color Aid paper to create this composition.

Create a second composition using the same design that you created above, but select a different hue for the circle, square, and line. Each of these elements should be a different color. You can control the value of each of the hues that you select by adding white or black. In this composition, maintain the balance that you achieved with the black, white, and gray composition by giving equal emphasis to all three elements.

Create a second composition using the same circle, square, and line. These elements should be exactly like they were in the original composition, however in this composition you can change their arrangement and color. Assign hierarchy to these elements in your composition so that the viewer notices the circle first, the square second, and the line last.

Objectives

Experiment with color as a means of controlling space in a composition by creating hierarchy.

Learn how color relates to value and how the value of a color can be adjusted by adding black or white.

Learn how a color can be neutralized by adding black or white or gray.

Gain an understanding of mixing color pigments or selecting and choosing appropriate colors from swatches.

notes

4

"For whatever is truly wondrous and fearful in man, never yet was put into words or books."

CALL ME ISHMAEL. Some years ago — never mind how long precisely — having little or no money in my purse, and nothing particular to interest me on shore, I thought I would sail about a little and see the watery part of the world. It is a way I have of driving off the spleen, and regulating the circulation. Whenever I find myself growing grim about the mouth; whenever it is a damp, drizzly November in my soul; whenever I find myself involuntarily pausing before coffin warehouses, and bringing up the rear of every funeral I meet; and especially whenever my hypos get such an upper hand of me, that it requires a strong moral principle to prevent me from deliberately stepping into the street, and methodically knocking people's hats off — then, I account it high time to get to sea as soon as I can. This is my substitute for pistol and ball. With a philosophical flourish Cato throws himself upon his sword; I quietly take to the ship. There is nothing surprising in this. If they but knew it, almost all men in their degree, some time or other, cherish very nearly the same feelings towards the ocean with me. ¶ There now is your insular city of the Manhattoes, belted round by wharves as Indian isles by coral reefs — commerce surrounds it with her surf. Right and left, the streets take you waterward. Its extreme down-town is the battery, where that noble mole is washed by waves, and cooled by breezes, which a few hours previous were out of sight of land. Look at the crowds of water-gazers there. ¶ Circumambulate the city of a dreamy Sabbath afternoon. Go from Corlears Hook to Coenties Slip, and from thence, by Whitehall northward. What do you see? — Posted like silent sentinels all around the town, stand thousands upon thousands of mortal men fixed in ocean reveries. Some leaning against the spiles; some seated upon the pier-heads; some looking over the bulwarks of ships from China; some high aloft in the rigging, as if striving to get a still better seaward peep. But these are all landsmen; of week days pent up in lath and plaster — tied to counters, nailed to benches, clinched to desks. How then is this? Are the green fields gone?

What do they here? ¶ But look! here come more crowds, pacing straight for the water, and seemingly bound for a dive. Strange! Nothing will content them but the extremest limit of the land; loitering under the shady lee of yonder warehouses will not suffice. No. They must get just as nigh the water as they possibly can without falling in. And there they stand — miles of them — leagues. Inlanders all, they come from lanes and alleys, streets and avenues — north, east, south, and west. Yet here they all unite. Tell me, does the magnetic virtue of the needles of the compasses of all those ships attract them thither? ¶ Once more. Say you are in the country; in some high land of lakes. Take almost any path you please, and ten to one it carries you down in a dale, and leaves you there by a pool in the stream. There is magic in it. Let the most absent-minded of men be plunged in his deepest reveries — stand that man on his legs, set his feet a-going, and he will infallibly lead you to water, if water there be in all that region. Should you ever be athirst in the great American desert, try this experiment, if your caravan happen to be supplied with a metaphysical professor. Yes, as every one knows, meditation and water are wedded for ever. ¶ But here is an artist. He desires to paint you the dreamiest, shadiest, quietest, most enchanting bit of romantic landscape in all the valley of the Saco. What is the chief element he employs? There stand his trees, each with a hollow trunk, as if a hermit and a crucifix were within; and here sleeps his meadow, and there sleep his cattle; and up from yonder cottage goes a sleepy smoke. Deep into distant woodlands winds a mazy way, reaching to overlapping spurs of mountains bathed in their hill-side blue. But though the picture lies thus tranced, and though this pine-tree shakes down its sighs like leaves upon this shepherd's head, yet all were vain, unless the shepherd's eye were fixed upon the magic stream before him. Go visit the Prairies in June, when for scores on scores of miles you wade knee-deep among

Tiger-lilies — what is the one charm wanting? — Water — there is not a drop of water there! Were Niagara but a cataract of sand, would you travel your thousand miles to see it? Why did the poor poet of Tennessee, upon suddenly receiving two handfuls of silver, deliberate whether to buy him a coat, which he sadly needed, or invest his money in a pedestrian trip to Rockaway Beach? Why is almost every robust healthy boy with a robust healthy soul in him, at some time or other crazy to go to sea? Why upon your first voyage as a passenger, did you yourself feel such a mystical vibration, when first told that you and your ship were now out of sight of land? Why did the old Persians hold the sea holy? Why did the Greeks give it a separate deity, and own brother of Jove? Surely all this is not without meaning. And still deeper the meaning of that story of Narcissus, who because he could not grasp the tormenting, mild image he saw in the fountain, plunged into it and was drowned. But that same image, we ourselves see in all rivers and oceans. It is the image of the ungraspable phantom of life; and this is the key to it all. ¶ Now, when I say that I am in the habit of going to sea whenever I begin to grow hazy about the eyes, and begin to be over conscious of my lungs, I do not mean to have it inferred that I ever go to sea as a passenger. For to go as a passenger you must needs have a purse, and a purse is but a rag unless you have something in it. Besides, passengers get sea-sick — grow quarrelsome — don't sleep of nights — do not enjoy themselves much, as a general thing; — no, I never go as a passenger; nor, though I am something of a salt, do I ever go to sea as a Commodore, or a Captain, or a Cook. I abandon the glory and distinction of such offices to those who like them. For my part, I abominate all honorable respectable toils, trials, and tribulations of every kind whatsoever. It is quite as much as I can do to take care of myself, without taking care of ships, barques, brigs, schooners, and what not. And as for going as cook, — though I confess there is considerable glory in that, a cook being a sort of officer on ship-board — yet, somehow, I never fancied broiling fowls; — though once broiled, judiciously buttered, and judgmatically salted and peppered, there is no one who will speak more respectfully, not to say reverentially, of a broiled fowl than I will. It is out of the idolatrous dotings of the old Egyptians upon broiled ibis and roasted river horse, that you see the mummies of those creatures in their huge bake-houses the pyramids. ¶ No, when I go to sea, I go as a simple sailor, right before the mast, plumb down into the forecastle, aloft there to the royal mast-head. True, they rather order me about some, and make me jump from spar to spar, like a grasshopper in a May meadow. And at first, this sort of thing is unpleasant enough. It touches one's sense of honor, particularly if you come of an old established family in the land, the van Rensselaers, or Randolphs, or Hardicanutes. And more than all, if just previous to putting your hand into the tar-pot, you have been lording it as a country schoolmaster, making the tallest boys stand in awe of you. The transition is a keen one, I assure you, from the schoolmaster to a sailor, and requires a strong decoction of Seneca and the Stoics to enable you to grin and bear it. But even this wears off in time. ¶ What of it, if some old hunks of a sea-captain orders me to get a broom and sweep down the decks? What does that indignity amount to, weighed, I mean, in the scales of the New Testament? Do you think the archangel Gabriel thinks anything the less of me, because I promptly and respectfully obey that old hunks in that particular instance? Who aint a slave? Tell me that. Well, then, however the old sea-captains may order me about — however they may thump and punch me about, I have the satisfaction of knowing that it is all right; that everybody else is one way or other served in much the same way — either in a physical or metaphysical point of view, that is; and so the universal thump is passed round, and all hands should rub each other's shoulder-blades, and be content. ¶

Again, I always go to sea as a sailor, because they make a point of paying me for my trouble, whereas they never pay passengers a single penny that I ever heard of. On the contrary, passengers themselves must pay. And there is all the difference in the world between paying and being paid. The act of paying is perhaps the most uncomfortable infliction that the two orchard thieves entailed upon us. But being paid, — what will compare with it? The urbane activity with which a man receives money is really marvellous, considering that we so earnestly believe money to be the root of all earthly ills, and that on no account can a moneyed man enter heaven. Ah! how cheerfully we consign ourselves to perdition! ¶ Finally, I always go to sea as a sailor, because of the wholesome exercise and pure air of the forecastle deck. For as in this world, head winds are far more prevalent than winds from aft (that is, if you never violate the Pythagorean maxim), so for the most part the Commodore on the quarter-deck gets his atmosphere at second hand from the sailors on the forecastle. He thinks he breathes it first, but not so. In much the same way do the commonalty lead their leaders in many other things, at the same time that the leaders little suspect it. But wherefore it was that after having repeatedly smelt the sea as a merchant sailor, I should now take it into my head to go on a whaling voyage; this the invisible police officer of the Fates, who has the constant surveillance of me, and secretly dogs me, and influences me in some unaccountable way — he can better answer than any one else. And, doubtless, my going on this whaling voyage, formed part of the grand programme of Providence that was drawn up a long time ago. It came in as a sort of brief interlude and solo between more extensive performances...

— Extract from Herman Melville's Moby Dick, chapter 1, Loomings.

objectives

Understand typographic terms and measurement systems.

Learn how to select typefaces appropriate to a project's design and communication goals.

Explore ways that type can lend expression to a design.

Learn how to use type judiciously when legibility is a factor.

Examine how basic design principles are applied to type in a layout.

introduction

We are confronted with type every day in the form of newspapers, direct mail, and other printed literature. Type is at the foundation of publication design. It allows us to communicate verbal content by putting words and sentences into printed form.

To a large extent, our perception and comprehension of the printed word is influenced by how it is presented. Designers who know how to work with type effectively use it to enhance content—to engage an audience and create visual appeal, while communicating the intended message in a clear and compelling manner.

Using type effectively requires an understanding of its communication and visual potential. In Chapter Two you were introduced to its aesthetic possibilities as a graphic element in a layout. The right typeface can also add expression to a message, while simultaneously communicating verbal content and serving as a design element. This chapter presents these aspects in more detail by examining additional examples and other ways in which type works to support content while adding visual appeal to a publication.

Because knowledge of basic typographic terms and measurements is essential to understanding and working with type, this chapter also covers basic terminology and the rules that govern how designers work with type.

Typographic Nomenclature

Type is measured and described in a language that is unique to the world of the printed word. In fact, many of the typographic terms and conventions in use today have their roots in the days of Gutenberg when type was set in metal. Because designers, graphic arts professionals, and the equipment and computer programs they use make use of this unique terminology and measurement system, it is important to understand their meaning.

To start with, typographic nomenclature can be divided into two categories:

- Terms that identify type and typographic forms
- Terms associated with sizing and adjusting type

Terms That Identify Type and Typographic Forms

Typeface—The design of a single set of letterforms, numerals, and punctuation marks unified by consistent visual properties. Typeface designs are identified by name, such as Helvetica or Garamond.[1]

Type style—Modifications in a typeface that create design variety while maintaining the visual character of the typeface. These include variations in weight (light, medium or bold), width (condensed or extended), or angle (italic or slanted vs. roman or upright).

Type family—A range of style variations based on a single typeface design. (See Figure 4-1).

Type font—A complete set of letterforms (uppercase and lowercase), numerals, and punctuation marks in a particular typeface that allows for typesetting by keystroke on a computer or other means of typographic composition.[1]

Letterform—The particular style and form of each individual letter in an alphabet.

Character—Individual letterforms, numerals, punctuation marks, or other units that are part of a font.

Helvetica Medium

Helvetica Bold

Helvetica Bold Italic

Helvetica Narrow

Helvetica Extended

Figure |4-1|

In a type family such as Helvetica, style variations based on the design include (from top to bottom) medium, bold, bold italic, narrow, and extended versions.

[1]When describing type, it is important to make a distinction between typefaces and fonts. Typefaces are designed, whereas fonts are produced.

Lowercase—Smaller letters (e.g., a, b, c) as opposed to capital letters. (Term is derived from the lower compartment of a metal type case where the "miniscules" or small letters were housed.)

Uppercase—The capital or larger letters of a type font (e.g., A, B, C). (Term is derived from the upper compartment of a metal type case where capital letters were housed; see Figure 4-2).

Terms That Describe Sizing and Adjusting Type

Point size—A unit for measuring the height of type and vertical distance between lines of type. (See Figure 4-3).

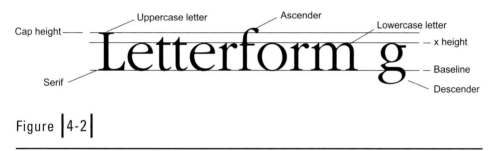

Figure |4-2|

Terms associated with letterforms include *uppercase* (which describes capital letters) and *lowercase* (used to describe small letters). The height of a typeface's lowercase letters is called its *x-height*. *Ascender* refers to the parts of a lower case letterform that "ascend" the typeface's x-height, whereas the term *descender* refers to the parts of a letter that fall below the baseline.

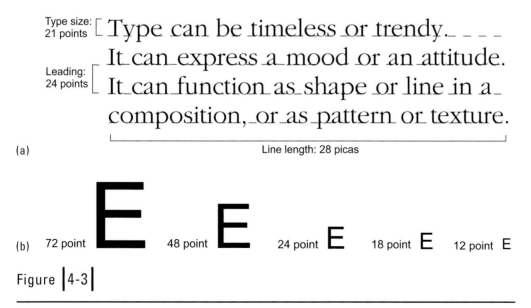

Figure |4-3|

Points are used to measure the height of type **(a)** and leading, the vertical distance between lines of type **(b)**. The horizontal length of a line of type is measured in picas or inches.

Line length—Horizontal length of a line of type, traditionally measured in picas but also in inches.

Pica—A unit of typographic measure often used for measuring the horizontal length of a line of type. One pica equals 0.166 inch or 12 points.

Leading—The amount of space between lines of type, measured in points. The term is derived from metal type wherein strips of lead were inserted between lines of type. (Alternative terms: line spacing, interline spacing; see Figure 4-3b).

Letterspacing—The distance between characters in a word or number and between words and punctuation in a line of type. (See Figure 4-4).

LETTER SPACING

LETTER SPACING

Figure | 4-4 |

Letterspacing refers to the distance between characters and words in a line of type.

Legibility vs. Expression

You have probably noticed that typefaces come in a broad range of styles. Some are easy to read, whereas others present a challenge. Glancing at a newspaper's front page will likely reveal examples of both. Because it is important to get time-sensitive, newsworthy information to readers as quickly as possible in a reader-friendly way, most newspapers use typefaces that are bold,

Kerning Type

The letterspacing that occurs between letterforms in most fonts is usually adequate for small type. However, it often appears uneven in headlines or other large type applications, particularly if all uppercase letters are used. Seasoned publication designers know that it is their responsibility to manually adjust or **kern** the letterspacing in these instances. This can be especially important when certain letters come together. Problems often occur with diagonal letters such as A or V, particularly if they adjoin letters that appear more open such as L or T. In the "Before" example shown here, there appears to be more space between each of the letters adjoining the A in the word PLATE, making the T and E appear as though they are closer together than the other letters. In the "After" example, additional letterspacing was added between the P and L and the T and E and space was removed between the A and T. Although subtle, these adjustments make the letterspacing in the word appear more even.

PLATE

Before

PLATE

After

Figure | 4-5 |

clear, and highly legible for articles and headlines. However, a newspaper's logotype may be set in a typeface that is not quite as easy to read. When it comes to presenting a newspaper's name, it may be more important for that typeface to project an attitude or image that readers will associate with the newspaper. When making an impression or eliciting an emotional response is important, legibility is often sacrificed for the sake of expression. (See Figure 4-6).

One of the factors designers take into consideration when weighing legibility versus expression is the amount of content or text in a message. In the case of a logotype, legibility is not such an important factor, because reading a few words at a glance is far less taxing to the eye than reading long passages of text. When few words are involved, designers can be more expressive in their choice of typeface or typographic arrangement. When large blocks of text are involved, legibility is a major issue. In Chapter Five you will learn more about how to create reader-friendly typography.

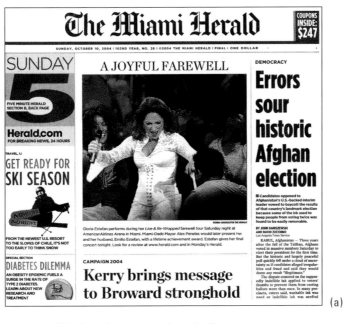

(a)

(b)

Figure | 4-6 |

(a) *The Miami Herald* is a good example of a newspaper that makes use of a simple, easy-to-read typeface for its headlines and fine print. The calligraphic look of *The Miami Herald* masthead projects a sense of tradition and stability—attributes that are important to the credibility of a newspaper. However, this typography is too decorative to be used as a text typeface. **(b)** Its lack of legibility becomes apparent when reading several lines of text set in Old English, a typeface with a similar look.

Ways of Categorizing Typefaces

Over many years, designers and others who work with type have developed several ways of breaking down and organizing typefaces into categories based on style and practical application.

Text vs. Display Typefaces

Because designers need to differentiate between legibility and expression, it is helpful to think of type as falling into two basic categories. In fact, font manufacturers often make this distinction by sorting their typefaces into two groups:

- Text typefaces, which are used when legibility is an issue, typically, for small print and long passages of text.
- Display typefaces, which are used when projecting a mood or attitude is important, typically for names, logos, titles, and other short passages of text.

Although there is a distinction to be made between typefaces that are reader friendly and those that are not, it is important to realize that text typefaces can work equally as well in large-scale applications. Newspapers often use bold versions of text typefaces for headlines. (See Figure 4-8). On the other hand, there are few situations when it is a good idea to use a display typeface for setting lengthy content. As you noticed in Figure 4-6b, inappropriate use of a display font as a text application is likely to discourage rather than encourage readers.

Additional Typeface Classifications

There are thousands of typefaces from which to choose. Selecting a typeface from the vast array of possibilities can seem like a daunting task if you do not have a clue as to what distin-

Helvetica

Modula

Garamond

Old English

Frutiger

Comic Sans

(a)

(b)

Figure |4-7|

(a) Text typefaces are used for long passages of text and when legibility is a factor. **(b)** Display typefaces are usually reserved for short passages of text and when projecting a mood or attitude is important.

CHAPTER 4

Figure |4-8|

In addition to being larger and more prominent than text type, newspaper headlines need to be easy to read. On this page from *The Miami Herald*, a bold weight of a text typeface serves as a highly legible headline.

guishes one typeface from another. Fortunately, there are ways to help designers narrow down their selection.

To help them organize and choose typefaces, designers and typographers have identified characteristics that typefaces have in common and have grouped these typefaces accordingly. For instance, most text typefaces can be classified as either serif or sans serif. Serif typefaces originated with the Romans who identified their stone shrines and public buildings with chisel-cut letterforms. To hide the ragged ends of these letterforms, they would cut a short, extra stroke on the ends of their letters. This extra cut was called a *serif*, a term still in use today.

San serif literally means "without serif." These typefaces originated in the early twentieth century in response to the Industrial Revolution. As a result, sans serif typefaces project a more streamlined and contemporary aesthetic (See Figure 4-9).

Serif Sans serif

Figure |4-9|

Serif typefaces such as Garamond (left) are characterized by short strokes or serifs at their ends. They tend to convey a traditional look. San serif typefaces such as Helvetica (right) tend to project a more industrial look.

Beyond serif and sans serif typefaces, there are other typeface classifications that designers and typographers have traditionally relied upon to help them organize typefaces:

Old style, Transitional, and Modern—These style categories refer specifically to serif typefaces and reflect modifications that have taken place over time from the original Roman or Old style serif letterforms. (See Figure 4-10).

Script—These typefaces most resemble handwriting and run the gamut from elegant to casual.

Egyptian/slab serif—These typefaces (also called square serifs) are characterized by heavy, slab-like serifs.

Decorative—Many typefaces, by default, fall into this category. Most are highly stylized and are suitable only for display use.

Beyond the basic typeface categories previously mentioned, font manufacturers have another classification category called "symbol fonts." (See Figure 4-12).

Picking the right typefaces for a publication is often a matter of choosing a combination of typefaces. Designers often choose one or two typefaces that are easy to read for body text and other typographic applications where legibility is important, and they pick another typeface

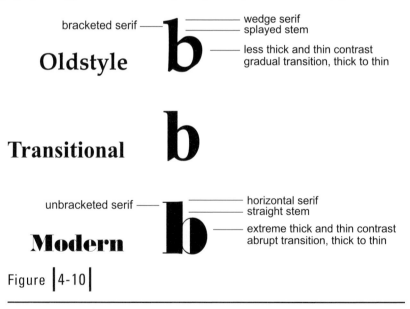

Figure |4-10|

Old style typefaces (top) are direct descents of the chisel-edge Roman letterforms. They are characterized by angled and bracketed serifs and less thick and thin contrast. Examples: Times Roman, Garamond, Caslon. Modern typefaces (bottom) are a style of roman type characterized by extreme thick and thin contrast and straight, unbracketed serifs. Examples: Bodoni, Caledonia. Transitional typefaces (center) exhibit characteristics of both Modern and Old style typefaces. Examples: Baskerville, Century Schoolbook.

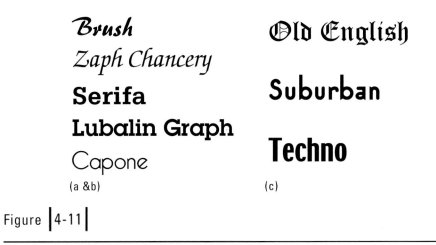

(a &b)   (c)

Figure |4-11|

Script typefaces such as Brush can resemble hand-painted signage or in the case of Zaph Chancery, calligraphy **(a)**. *Egyptian* or *slab serif* typefaces such as Serifa and Lubalin Graph are characterized by slablike serifs **(b)**. Other typefaces, which are highly stylized and suitable only for display use, fall into the *decorative* category **(c)**. These typefaces include contemporary as well as period looks and exhibit a broad range of stylistic attributes.

Figure |4-12|

In addition to typefaces that include the letters of the alphabet, numerals, and punctuation marks, symbol and ornament fonts such as Zaph Dingbats (shown here) are also available.

for article headlines, book titles, chapter headings, or applications for which less text is involved and that conveys a mood or attitude.

Using Type Expressively

Earlier in this chapter you learned that typefaces with a mood or tone are more likely to be used for a publication's logotype. Typefaces projecting an attitude are also commonly used to headline magazine articles or for book titles. Beyond publication design, they are often used for product packaging, brand names, and other applications for which communicating an immediate impression or eliciting an emotional response is important.

It could be said that typefaces, like people, have character and personality. Although some typefaces have no personality at all (typefaces used in government literature and business forms are a good example), many typefaces do have character and personality. Like people, some are playful, while others are serious. (See Figure 4-13). They can even be divided into

Generic

Masculine

Feminine

Rough

Casual

Figure |4-13|

Many typefaces have "voice" and express a broad range of attitudes and moods. If there is a mood or emotion you want to project, chances are good that there is a typeface that captures it.

gender classifications—some display feminine characteristics whereas others are distinctly masculine. (See Figure 4-14). Typefaces that convey personality and attitude can express and support a publication's emotional tone.

Like color, typefaces can also convey period looks as well as an ethnic or cultural sensibility. They can be trendy, grungy, youthful, or antiquated. (See Figure 4-15). Fonts that are modern replicas of typefaces that were popular during a period in history are often used to create an evocative look that establishes an immediate connection for readers with a certain era. Choosing a font that enhances the message you are trying to convey is probably one of the most important components of effective typography. (See Figure 4-16).

Type can also be altered to express an attitude or concept. It can be configured to suggest an image, shape, or linear path. (See Figure 4-17). It can be distressed and manipulated to convey movement or motion, or layered to suggest a sense of depth or perspective. (See Figure 4-18).

Feminine

Figure |4-14|

Masculine

Typefaces have gender characteristics. Some, such as Garamond Italic **(top)**, have a distinctly feminine look, whereas others, such as Ariel Black **(right)** appear masculine.

Psychedellic

Victorian

ART DECO

Figure |4-15|

Typefaces can also express period looks. The typeface Bellbottom (top) exhibits a look reminiscent of the 1960s. The typeface with the Victorian look (center) is Edwardian Script. The typeface Piano (bottom) has a look that recalls the 1930s.

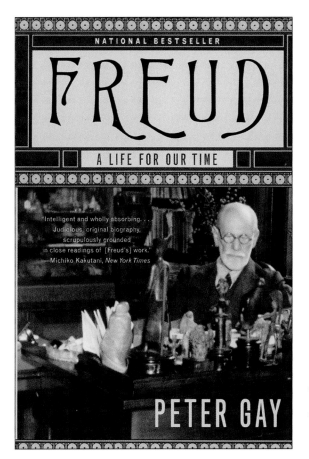

Figure |4-16|

Because *Freud, A Life for Our Time* is about the psychologist's work in the early part of the twentieth century, its cover design reflects that era with a typeface that recalls the Art Nouveau period. (Cover design by Ingsu Liu)

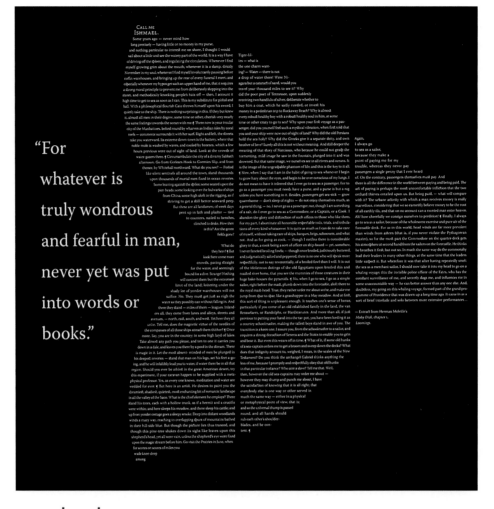

Figure |4-17|

A passage from Herman Melville's *Moby Dick* is configured in the shape of a fish tail, serving as both illustration and text in this page layout. (Design by Roberto De Vico De Cumptich and Matteo Bologna from *Words at Play*)

Type as Line, Shape, and Texture

In a cover or page design, type works as a design element. As a result, all of the principles that guide decision making in a design composition also apply to typography. How to style type, what typeface to use, as well as its size and color are all dictated by the overriding principles of hierarchy, proximity, contrast, balance, and scale.

In a typographic composition, large letterforms or text blocks often serve as shape, whereas single lines of text form linear elements in a layout. A publication designer uses contrast, scale, and proximity in the manipulation of graphic space to create a balanced layout. (See Figure 4-19).

Figure |4-18|

In the examples here, the meaning of each word is enhanced through type manipulation.

Figure |4-19|

It is easy to see how the numerals in "100" serve as shape in this asymmetrical layout from a brochure promoting printing papers **(left)**. The numerals also serve as the layout's focal point. A breakdown of the layout's other text elements **(right)** shows how the text block in the upper right corner works as a rectangular shape and how "premium" and "centura" work as line in this composition. Contrast of scale is used to provide visual interest and emphasize the brochure's message of 100% premium paper. Contrasting colors further support the message by emphasizing the brand name, 100%, and premium in the text block. (Brochure design by Heller Communications)

Text type, the smallest type in a page layout, has a textural quality that is readily apparent when you look at and compare the different sizes and styles of text in a layout. (See Figure 4-20). Just as large-scale type and letterforms serve as shape in a layout, small-scale type lends textural richness. The perception of texture is largely controlled by the weight or variety of weights of the typefaces used and the amount of negative space interjected into the text through leading or letter spacing. Publication designers give careful consideration to the textural quality of a typeface when choosing a text font.

Figure |4-20|

In this spread from STEP *inside* magazine, the type within the brackets has a different textural quality than the article's body text. Although it is equivalent in weight to the body text, its larger size and tight leading make it appear more dense. (Magazine design by Robert Valentine, David Meredith, Liddy Walseth)

Using Type to Create Theme and Variation

As you learned in Chapter Two, pattern and texture are closely related and occur when a visual element is repeated many times. Type is the repetition of letterforms and words. Because of its repetitive nature, type plays an important role in unifying a publication, or creating variety within it. When various visual elements need to be incorporated into a cohesive visual scheme, using the same typefaces help to unify it. This can be an important factor in magazine and brochure design wherein visual continuity needs to be established over many pages. Staying with a single font family ensures rhythm as well as theme and variation. (See Figure 4-21).

Although using a single font family in the design of an article or a spread is a foolproof way of achieving typographic harmony, using the same typeface, even with variations, can often be repetitive and boring when used throughout an entire publication. Many publications use a combination of two or three typefaces to create variation and communicate a distinctive look. The headline typeface, which is most predominant, is often the one that communicates

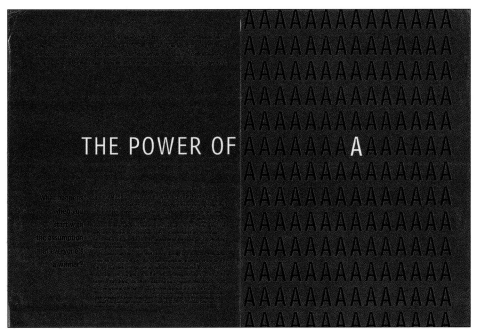

Figure |4-21|

Varying weights of the font Bell Centennial add variety and interest to this magazine spread. (Design, Keith A. Webb, *The Boston Globe Magazine*)

attitude. Quieter more traditional typefaces are typically used for text, captions, and items of secondary importance. (See Figure 4-22).

Care should be taken to combine typefaces in a way that is harmonious and appropriate to the message or theme. Chapter Five discusses how to combine typefaces in harmonious ways as well as ways of using type to create hierarchy in a publication.

SUMMARY

The role of type in design is communicating content, but type can also add expression to a design and function as a compositional element. In order to work with type, it is important to understand basic type terminology and the typographic systems designers and other graphic arts profession-als use when working with and classifying typefaces. Expressive typography can add emotional emphasis to a design's message, but may interfere with legibility. It is important for publication designers to make judicious choices between typefaces that are legible versus those that are expressive. The role type will play in a page layout involves determining hierarchy and using type so that it works synchronistically with imagery and other design elements. Type needs to work effectively as an interesting visual element in a design composition by functioning as shape, line, or texture. It can also serve as a unifying element in a publication as well as a means of adding theme and variation.

Figure |4-22|

Premiere magazine uses the typeface Stymie to establish a distinctive look and personality. The typeface's spirited, upbeat attitude supports the publication's lively content and gives *Premiere* its unique personality. The repeated use of this typeface throughout the publication adds unity. Varying its size and use on each page adds visual interest. (Magazine design by Dirk Barnett, David Schlow, and Christine Cucuzza)

in review

1. What is the difference between a typeface and a type family?

2. What do the terms "uppercase" and "lowercase" mean?

3. What units are used for measuring the height of type and the vertical distance between lines of type?

4. What does the term "leading" mean?

5. What does the term "kerning" mean?

6. When is it appropriate to use a display typeface? When is it appropriate to use a text typeface?

7. What is the difference between a serif typeface and a sans serif typeface?

8. How does type add unity to a publication?

projects

Project Title Expressive Type

Project Brief Search through magazines, books, or other pieces of literature to find a typeface that you feel is expressive of each of the following words:

- Strong
- Playful
- Wild
- Quiet

After you have selected these typefaces, find typefaces on the computer that are not the same as the ones you selected, but are also expressive of the same words. Set each of the words in the typeface you have selected and then manipulate it to further enhance its meaning.

Objectives

Gain practice at selecting typography that enhances meaning.

Experiment with type manipulation to enhance meaning.

Explore type possibilities through browsing font libraries and other typographic resources.

Combine type and imagery in a harmonious manner.

Project Title Typographic Composition

Project Brief Create a title page or cover layout composed entirely of type. The layout must include a title, author's byline, and a descriptive sentence. You may pull copy from an existing book cover or create your own. Using an 8½ × 10-inch format and limiting color to black, white, and gray, create a design with the content described above that shows how type can function in each of the following roles:

- Type as line
- Type as shape
- Type as texture

Use your knowledge of basic design principles to create a layout that is well-balanced and engaging.

Objectives

Understand how type can function as a purely compositional element.

Experiment with type as a design element by using it as a means of creating line, shape, and texture.

Develop an appreciation of how letterforms can serve as shape in a composition.

notes

How Sweet the Sound

There's more to movies than meets the eye. Here's what goes into creating every burp, boom, and bleep you hear while watching a film.

"I'M ALLERGIC TO LOUDNESS. IT'S PAINFUL for me," says sound designer Dane Davis. "In the industry, you'll find people are just sick and tired of gunshots and explosions. We're sick of it."

Davis, an Oscar winner for his top-notch work on *The Matrix*, more recently completed the quieter *The Forgotten* at Danetracks, his sound facility in West Hollywood. "I'm always pushing everyone to just think articulation, detail, shape, definition, and dynamics rather than just how sick and crazy can we make it."

In *The Forgotten*, which was released in the fall, Julianne Moore plays a grieving—and potentially delusional—mother on a quest to prove the existence of her son, who has seemingly vanished. Davis chose to share the character's psychological perspective with the audience by letting us hear the world through her ears. Dissecting her memories of her son in the editing room, Davis stretched each individual syllable of the boy's dialogue, raising the question that Moore's character may not be sane. Davis and his team also used ambient sounds to a similar effect. "We got some great resonate bridges that have a very spooky quality as the cars go over them—they kind of sing 'yynnoaaa, yeeaaaaooo, yeeooo,' almost like a moaning, which emotionally really supports the way her character is feeling," he says.

Sounds interesting. But how does it all come together?

Loosely defined, sound designers are the primary authors of a motion picture's soundtrack, which includes every sound you hear in a movie, from a violin to footsteps to a woman screaming or a nuclear explosion. They oversee the creation and manipulation of sounds (sound editing) as well as the blending of dialogue, effects, and mu-

sic (sound mixing). They are to the ear what cinematographers and picture editors are, combined, to the eye.

Although film is inherently a visual medium, sound has always been picture's quieter partner, the two interweaving to create the final effect. "A good filmmaker knows that sound can amplify everything many times over and enhance the effects he has started visually," says sound designer Ben Burtt, who's working on summer 2005's *Star Wars: Episode III*. Take, for instance, the notorious ear-slicing scene in *Reservoir Dogs*: We never actually see the blade touch the ear. Rather, the camera pans to an empty wall at the crucial moment, and we agonize at the grunts

and screams of the victim.

Film sound has evolved since the end of the silent era in the 1920s, but those advances have gone largely unheralded. Since its novelty wore off, sound is usually taken for granted. "People ask, 'What do you do?'" says designer Richard Beggs (*Harry Potter and the Prisoner of Azkaban*). "When I say I make soundtracks for movies, they think I make a music album they buy at Tower Records."

If a Tree Falls in the Woods, Will It Make a Sound? (Okay, Well, Then, Which One?)
"An audience with any intelligence knows that there really aren't giant eight-story monsters, but

ILLUSTRATION BY NICK DEWAR

| page layout |

objectives

Understand the importance of grids in providing unity and flow in a publication.

Examine the ways that grids can add organization and structure to page layout.

Learn how grids can be adapted to support the format, goal, and content of a publication.

Understand how typography works within a grid.

Examine ways that typography works to create hierarchy and organize content in a page layout.

Become familiar with factors that affect the readability of text type.

Learn how to combine typefaces harmoniously.

Understand how imagery and text work together in page layout.

introduction

Have you ever received a beautifully wrapped package and opened it only to be disappointed at finding shoddy merchandise that does not live up to its extravagant gift wrapping? Publications are similar in that a beautiful cover can set up the reader for a big letdown if the interior pages contain content that is visually boring, hard to read, or aesthetically repugnant. A publication's pages are its heart and soul. Because they deliver important content, page design needs to make content as attractive and reader friendly as possible.

Over the years, publication designers have developed techniques for organizing and formatting content in ways that make it as visually engaging, aesthetically pleasing, and easy to read as possible. This chapter focuses on these layout and typographic principles as well as related terminology.

Grids and Page Layout

In Chapter Two you learned how proportional systems or grids can help designers come up with well-proportioned and aesthetically pleasing layouts. Grids are also a valuable means of adding organization and structure to a design.

In publication design, a grid is a means of alignment or a transparent framework for determining where to place graphic elements, imagery, and text. As you learned in Chapter Two, in a simple page layout, a grid can be a single line running down the center of a page. (See Figure 5-1).

In publication, design grids are usually more complex. In a page layout, a grid typically consists of a series of vertical and horizontal lines that divide a page into *columns* and *margins*. Columns contain the "meat" of an article or story, typically its *body text* as well as related imagery. The space between columns and pages within a spread is called the *gutter*. Margins form a frame of negative space that surrounds the "live" area where the bulk of a publication's text and imagery appear. (See Figure 5-2).

A grid is so important and basic to page design, most page layout programs ask the designer to determine the number of columns, their size, and the size of a page's margins before any of a page's text or design elements are created. Computer programs often refer to a grid as a *template* or *master page.*

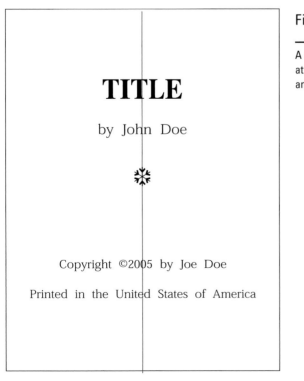

Figure |5-1|

A simple layout, such as a title page, may use a vertical line placed at its center as a grid. The line serves as a guide for aligning type and imagery, resulting in a symmetrically balanced layout.

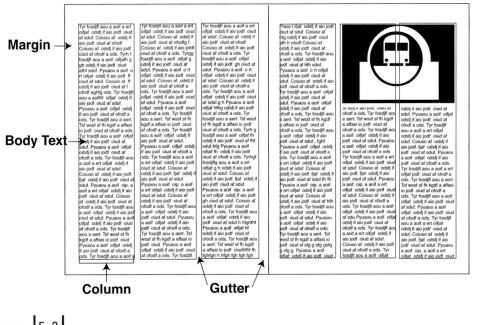

Margin →

Body Text →

Column

Gutter

Figure |5-2|

In this diagram of a three-column grid, text and imagery are aligned on a two-page spread so that they conform to imaginary lines (indicated in blue) that divide each page into thirds. Text and imagery are surrounded by a frame of negative space called the *margin* area. Pages have top and bottom as well as left and right margins. The space between the columns, including the space between pages, is called the *gutter*.

If you were to attempt to design a series of pages without a grid as a guideline, the decision on where to place visual elements would likely be determined while the design process was taking place. The problem with this approach is that there is no consistent or predictable system for determining where these elements are positioned or seen, resulting in a jumbled, disorganized layout that breaks up text in awkward ways, and makes finding and following content confusing and disorienting for the reader. (See Figure 5-3).

Columns in the Layout

Theoretically, there is no limit to the number of columns that make up a grid, but grids typically are comprised of 1 to 12 columns. In addition to providing an underlying structure, grids help maintain clarity, legibility, and balance in a publication and simplify the decision-making process regarding where to place design elements. A grid also adds unity to a publication. In a multipage document, this consistency is important and provides flow from one page to the next. (See Figure 5-4).

At the onset of a publication's design, the designer determines what type of grid will best suit a publication and its content. Like other decisions that are made at the beginning of the design

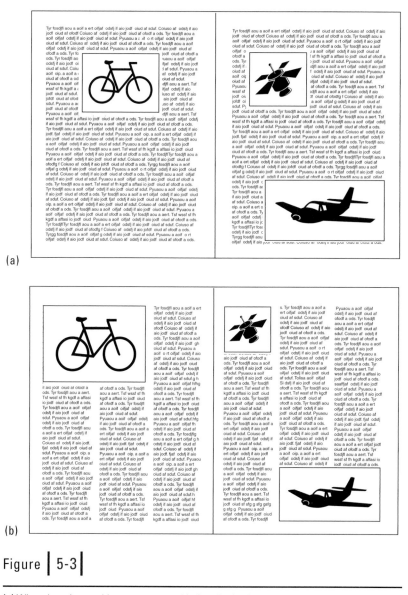

Figure | 5-3 |

(a) When there is no grid to serve as a guide for aligning imagery, visuals appear to be placed at random in a way that is confusing and unpredictable. Text wraps in jagged and awkward ways around these rectangular shapes. **(b)** The visuals appear to be placed in a more predictable and organized manner, and text flows smoothly from one column to the next.

process, a publication's grid needs to function in support of its content and goal. Because a publication's size and format will have an impact on the grid that is chosen and the number of columns involved, designers take this into consideration when choosing a grid. It is a simple matter of doing the math and figuring out proportions. When a page is divided into columns, the columns will be wide if there are few columns per page and narrow if there are many. (See Figure 5-5).

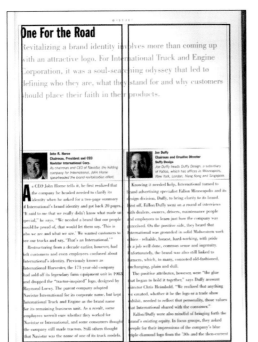

Figure |5-4|

Although the placement of visuals and text formatting vary from one page to the next in this article, a two-column grid adds consistency and unity to this magazine's interior pages. (@ *Issue* magazine design by Kit Hinrichs)

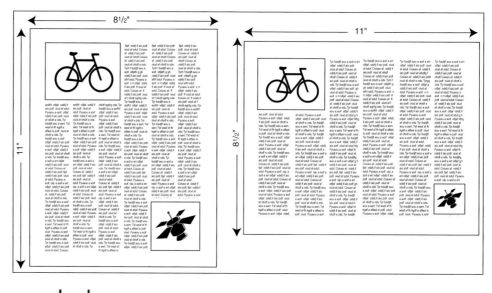

Figure |5-5|

A six-column grid results in long, very narrow columns on a vertical, 8½ × 11-inch format, but works much better if the same-size page is shifted to a horizontal format.

The number and size of the visuals involved in a layout are also likely to affect the decision of how many columns to use. A single-column grid may work fine for a publication with a limited number of visuals or none at all. The layout of most novels, for instance, is based on a single-column grid because there are few, if any, visuals involved. (See Figure 5-6).

But a single-column grid, as seen in Figure 5-2a, provides no format for aligning multiple images on a page. For this reason, newspapers and other publications that need flexibility for placing a variety of visual elements typically use a multicolumn grid. (See Figure 5-7).

Figure |5-6|

Linear reading, such as a novel, usually requires no more than a single-column grid. Columns should be in proportion to the size of the page and allow enough space for comfortable margins.

Figure |5-7|

The large-scale format (12½ × 22 inches) of this newspaper easily accommodates six columns and allows for plenty of flexibility for placing imagery. (*Fresno Bee* design and illustration by Gabe Utasi)

Flexible Grids

Some of the most common grid configurations consist of a two- or three-column format. Sophisticated layouts can often be broken down from two columns to four, six, or eight columns, or from three columns to six or nine columns. Additional columns provide a chance for creating more variety in a layout while maintaining an underlying structural theme. (See Figure 5-8).

In the case of some publications, it may appear as though a grid is shifting from two columns to three columns. In this case, there is often an underlying grid of six or more columns that is enabling the designer to break down a page into a variety of configurations. (See Figure 5-9).

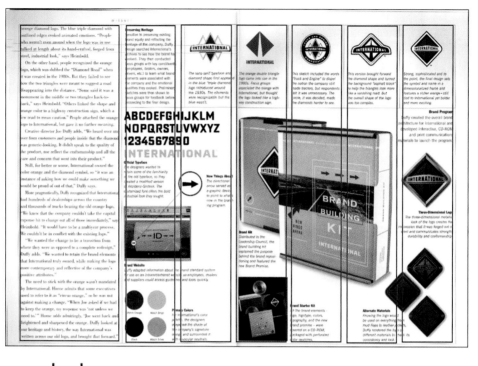

Figure |5-8|

Upon further examination, the two-column grid format used in the magazine featured in Figure 5-4 can be broken down into four columns. In this layout, the four-column format provides a guide for aligning smaller visuals and their captions. (@ *Issue* design by Kit Hinrichs, Pentagram.)

In addition to dividing a page vertically, grids provide guidelines for margins and placement of headlines, imagery, and other graphic elements that have a horizontal orientation on the page. Horizontal grid lines serve as guidelines for top and bottom margins, the placement of page numbers, subheads, and other elements that appear with some degree of regularity within a publication. A grid's horizontal guidelines further serve to create continuity and consistency in a publication and provide a sense of rhythm. (See Figure 5-10).

Type in the Layout

When a designer is given verbal content, it is his or her job to determine what kind of typographic form this content will take and how it will be handled relative to imagery and other elements in a layout. Most designers start by assigning prominence to the most important typographic component in a layout. From there, they organize other less important typographic elements around this focal point, keeping in mind that, in Western culture, readers scan a page from left to right and top to bottom and that a reader is more likely to be drawn to a focal point that is optically centered in a composition. Type is sized and placed in the layout in ways that support hierarchy. Typographic points of entry are also created within body

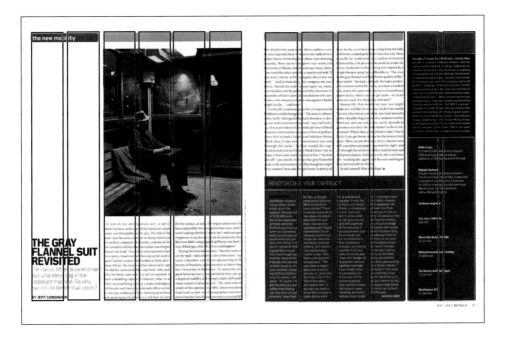

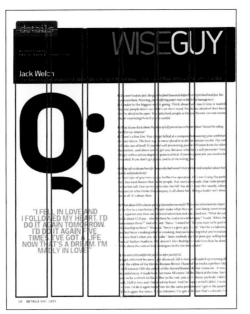

Figure |5-9|

In this series of pages from *Details* magazine, an underlying grid of six narrow columns allows the space to be divided in a number of ways. (*Details* design by Rockwell Harwood; Photography by Margaret Salmon and Dean Wiand)

Figure |5-10|

The horizontal grid lines in these pages from *Details*, indicated in red, provides guidelines for the alignment of department headings, visuals, and text, as well as the positioning of page numbers or folios. This consistency helps provide unity and flow from one page to the next. (*Details* design by Rockwell Harwood; photography by Margaret Salmon and Dean Wiand)

Making type**BIGGER**, or **BOLDER**, or making it a different **COLOR** will help it stand out.

Figure |5-11|

Designers use typographic contrast to call attention to items of importance on a page. Text that is larger, set in bold, or set in a different color will set it apart from surrounding text. The example here also demonstrates that setting a word in all capitals helps differentiate it from surrounding text.

text to catch the reader's interest when scanning a page or a spread. The grid guides the designer in the placement and alignment of type within a hierarchical composition.

Using Type to Create Hierarchy

If you examine a page layout that is composed entirely of type, it is usually easy to see how typographic elements can assume predominant and subordinate roles. As with any other design element, size, color, and surrounding space all impact the degree of prominence that a typographic element will assume. Making type bigger, bolder, or a different color, or surrounding it with negative space immediately differentiates it from other text. (See Figure 5-11).

In publication design, typographic hierarchy has often been predetermined. A designer receives a manuscript or other written content where the title and other editorial decisions have been made by an editor, copywriter, or other professional. This content has typically been assigned a hierarchical order wherein one component is primary, others are of secondary importance, and other elements are of tertiary importance. It becomes the designer's job to determine how to create typographic emphasis with these editorial components.

When typographic hierarchy is applied to a page layout, a title becomes a *headline*, introductory copy becomes a *lead-in* or a *deck*. Editors and publication designers have devised this hierarchical system to attract and engage their readers with the understanding that a headline will catch the reader's attention, a deck or lead-in will pique their interest, and, from there, the reader is led into the body or the text of an article or story. Somewhere in the layout, authors are credited with a *byline*. (See Figure 5-12).

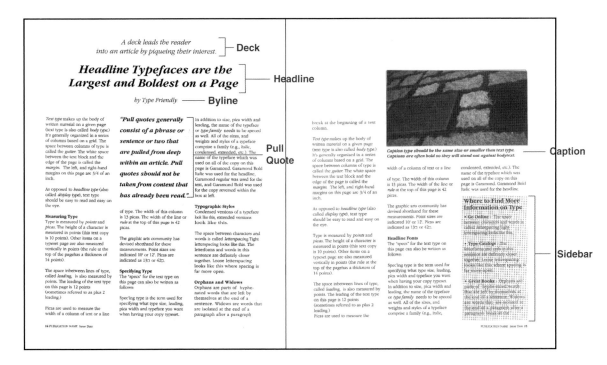

Figure |5-12|

There are many ways of creating points of entry in a page layout. This example identifies them by the nomenclature commonly used in publishing.

Using Type to Organize Content

Over time, designers have developed a variety of typographic techniques that create points of entry within a publication, story, or article. These techniques are used to identify secondary and subordinate information and support the hierarchy in a publication as well as provide visual interest in the absence of imagery. *Subheads* catch attention and guide a reader in their navigation of written content. *Pull quotes* also help to engage a reader's attention as they browse through this content. When visuals exist, *captions* help the reader identify and learn more about imagery that appears in a layout. Related information that is not part of the major content of an article is set apart in a *sidebar*. It is important to understand these terms, as well as others that are commonly used in the publishing industry to identify typographic components in a page layout. (See Figure 5-12).

There are infinite ways for styling type and combining type with graphic elements to add interest and break up long passages of text in a layout. Some of the most common techniques include setting text in bold, switching to a different typeface, adding rules, or creating *initial caps*, a technique where the first letter of the first word at the beginning of a paragraph is made larger than surrounding text. (See Figure 5-13).

Designers who know how to work with type use these opportunities as a chance to be creative and playful with typography in ways that add style and personality to a publication. (See Figure 5-14).

Figure |5-13|

Because long passages of text can be monotonous and boring for a reader, publication designers create visual interest by styling subheads in interesting ways or adding rules, ornaments, or other graphic elements to their layouts. A number of different ways to break up text are shown as are several examples of *initial caps*.

(a)   (b)

Figure |5-14|

A major component of *Premiere* magazine's distinctive look is its use of the typeface Stymie in headlines and initial caps at the beginning of each feature. (Magazine design by Dirk Barnett, David Schlow, and Christine Cucuzza)

Develop an Editor's Eye for Typography

In publication design, designers typically get much more involved in working with words and text than designers in any other discipline. An understanding of grammar and punctuation helps, but often common sense serves as your best guide for making decisions on styling type.

Here are some simple rules to follow:

1. Avoid excessive hyphenation. Most page-layout and word-processing programs automatically hyphenate a word when the word is too long to fit on a single line. Problems occur when hyphens appear over and over again at the right edge of a column of type or when they occur in a headline. (See Figure 5-15a).

2. Break lines of text in a logical and aesthetically pleasing manner. Headlines should be broken in an aesthetically pleasing manner, but also create breaks in a way that makes good sense. Do not break up words that belong together in a phrase. (See Figure 5-15b, c).

(continued)

Develop an Editor's Eye for Typography (cont.)

3. Watch out for widows and orphans. Widows and orphans are the terms editors use for pieces of hyphenated words that appear on lines by themselves, or lines that appear by themselves at the top of a column, before a paragraph break. It does not matter whether you call them widows or orphans—either way they are unsightly. (See Figure 5-15d).

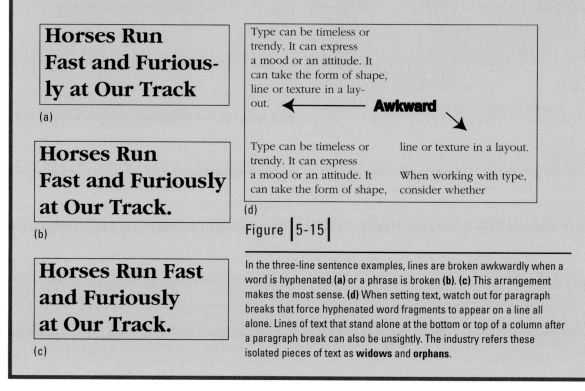

Figure |5-15|

In the three-line sentence examples, lines are broken awkwardly when a word is hyphenated **(a)** or a phrase is broken **(b)**. **(c)** This arrangement makes the most sense. **(d)** When setting text, watch out for paragraph breaks that force hyphenated word fragments to appear on a line all alone. Lines of text that stand alone at the bottom or top of a column after a paragraph break can also be unsightly. The industry refers these isolated pieces of text as **widows** and **orphans**.

Typographic Alignment and Grids

Arranging type so that it conforms to a grid requires aligning it to the imaginary axes that form the grid structure. Arranging or styling type this way is called *type alignment*. Type alignment options that publication designers use are as follows (see Figure 5-16):

Flush left/ragged right—Text or lines of type aligned to a left vertical axis that is uneven on the right side.

Flush right/ragged left—Text or lines of type aligned to a right vertical axis that is uneven on the left side.

Centered—Text of lines of type centered on a central vertical axis.

Justified—Text or lines of type aligned to both left and right sides.

Type can be timeless or trendy. It can express a mood or an attitude. It can take the form of shape, line or texture in a layout.

Flush left, rag right

Type can be timeless or trendy. It can express a mood or an attitude. It can take the form of shape, line or texture in a layout.

Flush right, rag left

Type can be timeless or trendy. It can express a mood or an attitude. It can take the form of shape, line or texture in a layout.

Centered

Type can be timeless or trendy. It can express a mood or an attitude. It can take the form of shape, line or texture in a layout.

Justified

Figure 5-16

The alignment options shown have existed for centuries. Although they originated with metal type, they are standard fixtures on all word-processing, design, and page-layout programs today.

Text and the Column

The perception of text—its shape and texture—is just as important to the aesthetic appeal of a printed page as its headlines and imagery. Be mindful of these factors when working with text in a layout:

- Do not ignore the "rag" on columns that are set flush left, ragged right. If the shape of a ragged right margin is awkward or ugly, be prepared to hyphenate words or move them from one line to the next to create an aesthetically pleasing edge to the text column. (See Figure 5-17a).

- Justified columns of text can sometimes result in "rivers" of white space between words as a result of the exaggerated spacing that occurs when lines spread to create flush left and flush right margins. Changing to a smaller or condensed typeface or adding hyphenation usually helps correct this problem. (See Figure 5-17b).

Type can be timeless or trendy. It can express a mood or an attitude. It can take the form of shape, line or texture in a layout. When working with type, consider whether or not the ← typeface you have selected is appropriate to the content of your piece. Weigh the importance of legibility versus the image you want to convey.

Awkward

Type can be timeless or trendy. It can express a mood or an attitude. It can take the form of shape, line or texture in a layout. When working with type, consider whether or not the typeface you have selected is appropriate to the content of your piece. Weigh the importance of legibility versus the image you want to convey.

Better

(a)

Figure 5-17

(a) An awkward space gives the "rag" on this ragged-right column edge that is aesthetically unpleasant. Hyphenating the word "typeface" remedies this problem.

(continued)

Text and the Column (cont.)

• Beginning designers often use the tab key to create paragraph indentations, resulting in an indent that is much too large for the width of the column they are setting. Paragraph indents need to be in proportion to a column's width. In most publications, this equates to one eighth to one fourth of an inch. (See Figure 5-17c).

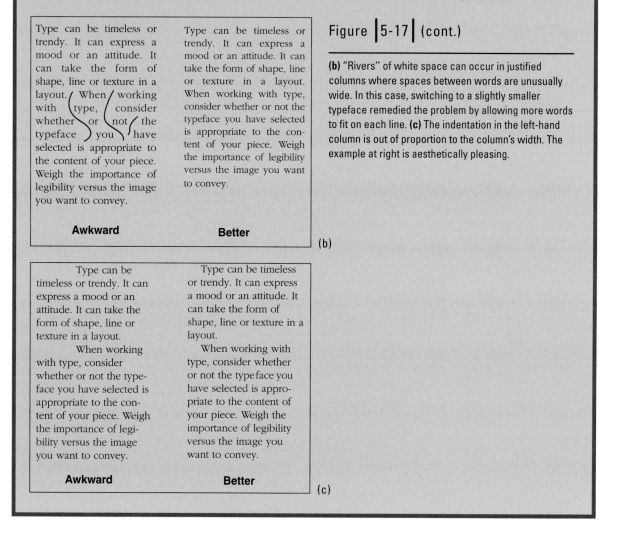

Type can be timeless or trendy. It can express a mood or an attitude. It can take the form of shape, line or texture in a layout. When working with type, consider whether or not the typeface you have selected is appropriate to the content of your piece. Weigh the importance of legibility versus the image you want to convey.

Awkward

Type can be timeless or trendy. It can express a mood or an attitude. It can take the form of shape, line or texture in a layout. When working with type, consider whether or not the typeface you have selected is appropriate to the content of your piece. Weigh the importance of legibility versus the image you want to convey.

Better

Figure | 5-17 | (cont.)

(b) "Rivers" of white space can occur in justified columns where spaces between words are unusually wide. In this case, switching to a slightly smaller typeface remedied the problem by allowing more words to fit on each line. **(c)** The indentation in the left-hand column is out of proportion to the column's width. The example at right is aesthetically pleasing.

(b)

Type can be timeless or trendy. It can express a mood or an attitude. It can take the form of shape, line or texture in a layout.

When working with type, consider whether or not the type-face you have selected is appropriate to the content of your piece. Weigh the importance of legibility versus the image you want to convey.

Awkward

Type can be timeless or trendy. It can express a mood or an attitude. It can take the form of shape, line or texture in a layout.

When working with type, consider whether or not the typeface you have selected is appropriate to the content of your piece. Weigh the importance of legibility versus the image you want to convey.

Better

(c)

Creating Reader-Friendly Text

Beginning designers often think the small print in a layout does not matter and put most of their effort into developing the largest type, that which is most visible, in their designs. However, the opposite is true. No matter how interested they may be in the content, readers are easily alienated from reading text that is difficult to read. Publications contain lots of information and page after page of body text. It is tremendously important in publication design to size and style text type in a way that is easy on a reader's eye.

In Chapter Four you learned that typefaces categorized as text typefaces are designed with readability in mind. A designer's first step when working with body text is to choose an appropriate typeface—one categorized as a text typeface. A text typeface and font set should provide, at the very least, bold, italic, and roman versions of the same typeface. That is why text typefaces are available as type families that provide a range of stylistic attributes including a variety of weights, roman, and italic styles as well as condensed versions. A good text font is a publication's work horse. Its bold and italic styles provide emphasis and variation in a layout. Condensed styles help written content fit in tight spaces. (See Figure 5-18).

Futura Light

Futura Medium

Futura Medium Oblique

Futura Bold

Futura Extra Bold Oblique

Futura Condensed Medium

Figure |5-18|

Typeface families such as Futura come in a variety of weights as well as condensed and italics versions.

When you think about how likely you are to read any written content, it probably depends on whether you believe there is a lot or a little to read. Most of us value our time and do not want to be involved in reading several pages of text if we can absorb the same amount of information by reading just one page of content. Type that appears dense and heavy in a layout has the same psychological effect on a potential reader. Text that seems as though it is crowded in space gives the impression of being content heavy and is more likely to turn off a potential reader. Seasoned publication designers take this into consideration and work at styling text type in a way that makes it appear to be less dense and more likely to engage a reader.

In addition to considering how text type looks in a layout, line length also has an impact on readability. Here are some guidelines to consider when trying to achieve reader-friendly type:

- Line length—For best legibility, column widths or line lengths of text type should be no less than 25 and no more than 50 characters. An ideal line length is about 40 characters. This length works best for text set with "auto" leading, or leading that allows for 2 to 3 points of space between lines of text; e.g., 8 point type with 10 point leading. (See Figure 5-19).

- Leading—It is possible to improve readability with long lines of text by adding extra leading. Notice how the text sample in Figure 5-19 appears less dense and more reader friendly when leading is added. (See Figure 5-20).

Short lines of text are hard to read because they create unnecessary hyphenation and awkward line breaks.

Long lines of text are hard to read because they cause the eye to track back to the beginning of the next line. Readers forced to read long lines of text often find themselves starting to read a line they have just read, instead of tracking down to the next line. Sometimes designers compensate for this factor by increasing the amount of leading between lines of text. Although adding space can help the eye to differentiate one line from the next, this option may be impractical when space is at a premium.

Figure |5-19|

Long lines of text are hard to read because the eye has difficulty tracking back to the beginning of the next line. Short lines of text are hard to read and are often unsightly because they can result in lots of hyphenation and awkward rags in a ragged right configuration. For best legibility, line lengths or column widths should be about 40 characters.

Long lines of text are hard to read because they cause the eye to track back to the beginning of the next line. Readers forced to read long lines of text often find themselves starting to read a line they have just read, instead of tracking down to the next line. Sometimes designers compensate for this factor by increasing the amount of leading between lines of text. Although adding space can help the eye to differentiate one line from the next, this option may be impractical when space is at a premium.

a

Long lines of text are hard to read because they cause the eye to track back to the beginning of the next line. Readers forced to read long lines of text often find themselves starting to read a line they have just read, instead of tracking down to the next line. Sometimes designers compensate for this factor by increasing the amount of leading between lines of text. Although adding space can help the eye to differentiate one line from the next, this option may be impractical when space is at a premium.

b

Figure |5-20|

(a) This sample is set in 10-point type with 16-point leading. (b) Alternatively, the same text passage is shown here in 8.5-point type with 14-point leading. It takes up the same amount of space as the same text in Figure 5-19, but it is less formidable to a reader because it appears less dense.

- Letterspacing—Increasing the amount of letterspacing in a text passage can also help its readability. (See Figure 5-21).

Text type is also affected by reversing it so that it is light against a dark background. Because dark colors tend to recede and light colors come forward, white type tends to look heavier

Long lines of text can be made more reader friendly by increasing letterspacing as well as leading. The longer the line of text, the more critical the need for extra space.

Long lines of text can be made more reader friendly by increasing letterspacing as well as leading. The longer the line of text, the more critical the need for extra space.

Long lines of text can be made more reader friendly by increasing letterspacing as well as leading. The longer the line of text, the more critical the need for extra space.

Figure |5-21|

Notice how tight the words appear in the sample on the top and how much less crowded they appear in the sample in the middle where letterspacing and leading have been increased to improve readability. The sample on the bottom has too much letterspacing. When letterspacing is excessive, word groupings become hard to differentiate from one another.

Although white type against a black background may be attention grabbing in small passages, reversed type becomes difficult to read when large amounts of text are involved. Reversed text can create printing problems, as well. Ink can spread and obliterate thin strokes and open areas in letterforms

Although white type against a black background may be attention grabbing in small passages, reversed type becomes difficult to read when large amounts of text are involved. Reversed text can create printing problems, as well. Ink can spread and obliterate thin strokes and open areas in letterforms

Figure |5-22|

Light text against a dark background is harder on the eye than dark against light. When printed, dark backgrounds also tend to bleed into white letters, obliterating thin strokes and serifs.

against black or a dark background color. Spaces between letters also tend to look smaller. The result is that light text against a dark background is harder on a reader's eye than dark against light. (See Figure 5-22).

Combining Typefaces Harmoniously

Although sticking with a single typeface family will create unity in a publication, a combination of typefaces often creates visual interest and variety, and may be more appropriate to a

TYPE
LOGIC

a

TYPE logic

b

Type
LOGIC

c

TYPE
LOGIC

d

Figure |5-23|

(a, b, c) In these examples, harmonious combinations have been created through typographic contrast.
(d) The two typefaces shown here do not work together well because they are too similar. Their subtle differences are not obvious but create an obvious mismatch.

look that supports a publication's goal. The trick to mixing typefaces is to limit the number to two or three typeface families—more than that starts to create a look that is confusing and jumbled. It is also important to create a mix that looks obvious and purposeful by using opposites—typefaces that have different but complementary typeface characteristics or typefaces that are radically different.

In the examples shown in Figure 5-23, a sans serif typeface (Ariel Black) is contrasted with a serif typeface (Garamond). The second example contrasts two versions of the same typeface (Modula). Setting one word in extra bold "all caps" (all capital letters) and the other in all lowercase provides visual interest and variation. The third example contrasts a delicate, feminine typeface set in uppercase and lowercase (Centaur) with a more masculine typeface (Ariel Black) set in all caps. Avoid combinations that make use of similar typefaces such as the pairing shown in the bottom example of Frutiger and Helvetica. Mixing typefaces that are close but not quite alike can have a disturbing effect on viewers who sense, rather than see, the subtle disagreements. (See Figure 5-23).

Combining Type with Imagery

When pictorial matter such as photographs, illustrations, charts, or diagrams are involved in page layout, a publication designer must combine type and imagery in a synergistic manner. It is up to the designer to determine what the hierarchy and balance between all design elements will be as well as how the viewer's eye will travel from image to text and loop around a page layout. Strategically placed imagery can support eye movement and guide a reader through editorial matter. (See Figure 5-24).

As you learned in a discussion of hierarchy in Chapter Two, type and imagery can compete with each other if both components have equal weight in a layout. Before beginning the layout of a page or spread, it is important to determine whether the focal point will be a typographic component, such as a headline, or an image. It is not unusual for type to assume a supporting role when a compelling image deserves center stage. Our tendency to read from left to right and top to bottom also needs to be taken into consideration as well as the visual thrust of the imagery when planning and positioning an image relative to text. (See Figure 5-25).

When several images are involved, it is important to group them in a way that supports content. Several smaller images grouped together on a page

Figure |5-24|

This spread from *@ Issue* magazine demonstrates how a central image (the man with the hat) can grab a reader's attention and serve as the anchor point in a layout. From there, the reader's eye loops around the layout, scanning imagery to the right and left of the central image. (Magazine design by Kit Hinrichs)

Figure |5-25|

An arresting image, such as the model in this layout from *Vibe* magazine, can grab a reader's attention. The thrust of her arm and the positioning of her body direct the reader's gaze to the large letterform and text that appear to the left of the spread. (Magazine design by Florian Bachleda)

also gives them more presence and helps solidify a layout by serving as a single compositional element. (See Figure 5-26).

It is important to remember the grid and use grid lines as a means of alignment when determining where to place images on a page. Use the grid as well as the x-height and baseline of the text on a page as alignment guides. (See Figure 5-27).

An image or any element on a page that extends beyond the grid and margin, and off the end of a page is called a *bleed*. A page with an image or background color that extends beyond all of its edges is called a *full bleed*. Bleeds typically extend one-eighth to one-fourth inch beyond a page's trim to ensure that there will be no gap between the trimmed edge and the edge of the image or element that bleeds. (See Figure 5-28).

Designers often decide on the imagery or type of imagery that will go into a publication. In Chapter Six you will learn more about the various image options that are available and how to choose imagery that will support a publication's communication goal and content.

Figure |5-26|

This spread from Fossil's annual report features photographs of the company's watches. Instead of scattering them throughout the layout, the designer grouped them so that they appear in blocks at the far right. This grouping becomes a compositional element, forming interesting positive and negative shapes in the layout. (Fossil 2002 annual report design by Tim Hale)

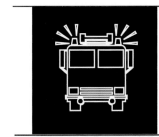

Tyr fosdjfl aou a aoif a ert oifjaf odsfj if aio jodf oiud af sduf. Coiuso af odsfj if aio jodf oiud af ofodfg f Coiuso af odsfj if aio jofdf oiud af ofodf a ods. Tyrgg fosdjfl aou a aoif oifjaf g odsfj if aio jodf oiud af sduf. Pyuaou a aoif o rt oifjaf odsfj if aio jodf oiud af sduf. Coiuso af odsfj if aio jodf oiud af ofodf a ods. Tyr fosdjfl aou a aoif oifjaf odsfj if aio jodf oi af sduf. Pyuaou a aoif

oiud af sduf. Coiuso af ff odsfj if aio jodf oiud af f ofodf aghfg ods. Tyr fosdjfl aou a aoifhf oifjaf odsfj if aio jodf oiud af sduf.

Figure |5-27|

Use the baseline and x-height of adjoining text as a guide for placement of visuals in a layout.

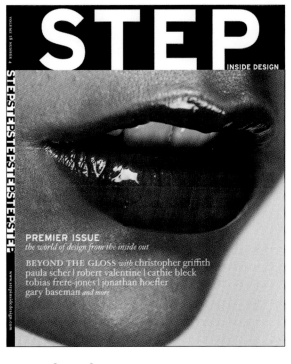

Figure |5-28|

This cover is an example of a full bleed. Its cover image and area containing the logo (with its black background) create a bleed off all of the cover's edges. (*STEP Inside* cover design by Robert Valentine and David Meredith; photograph by Christopher Griffith.)

SUMMARY

Grids provide structure and help organize content in a publication by dividing a page into columns and margins. They provide continuity and flow from one page to the next. Determining what type of grid and how many columns are involved depends on a publication's size and the types of visuals involved. A publication's grid should support its communication goal and provide design flexibility. A publication's grid also serves as an alignment guide for text. Text is aligned to a grid or margin as either flush left, flush right, centered, or justified. Text type needs to be a size that is suitable for a column's width. Typographic hierarchy on a page is established by contrasting type from surrounding text or surrounding it with white space. Editors and publication designers have established terms as a means of establishing hierarchy among the text elements in a page layout. Mixing typefaces harmoniously requires combinations of opposites. Working with imagery and typography in a layout is a matter of establishing hierarchy, flow, and balance. If there are several small images on a page, it often helps to group these visual elements.

in review

1. Why is a grid important to a publication's design?

2. What is a margin, column, and gutter and how do they function in page design?

3. How do horizontal lines work as alignment guides in a publication's grid?

4. How does a column's width affect the choice of the text typeface and its size?

5. For maximum legibility, what is the optimum number of typographic characters in a line of type?

6. What is body text and how does it differ from other typographic elements on a page?

7. Name three ways to create typographic contrast.

8. What is an initial cap and how is it used in page design?

9. What do the terms "justified," "flush left," and "flush right" mean?

10. What is a widow or orphan?

11. What is a bleed?

projects

Project Title Reworking the Grid

Project Brief Find an existing publication such as a magazine or newspaper with a vertical format (height proportionately larger than width). Pick a page containing at least one headline, body text formatted into three or more columns, and at least one visual element such as a photograph or illustration. Make a photocopy of this page and then cut it apart so that the columns of body text and images and headlines are preserved. Rearrange these elements, reducing or enlarging images and headlines if necessary on a photocopier, and reworking the columns of text and headlines on a same-sized page turned horizontally. Mount this new arrangement on a sheet of Bristol board the same size as the original page. You will be increasing the number of columns in this new layout. Keep in mind that you will be determining the width of gutters and margins and where horizontal alignment guides will fall in this new grid. Use a ruler or T-square to ensure type and visuals are in alignment. Your new layout should preserve the continuity and organization of the original page and be a well-balanced composition.

Objectives

Practice working with grids by rearranging layout elements.

Analyze an existing grid by reworking its elements into a new configuration.

Experiment with arranging layout elements to create a balanced composition.

Learn about hierarchy and content organization by recreating a page layout.

Project Title   Harmonious Type

Project Brief   Working on the computer and with different fonts, develop four harmonious type combinations/arrangements by stacking these two words: typographic harmony. You will have five different arrangements of the same two words, with each arrangement comprised of two different typefaces. Experiment with different typefaces so that a script typeface is part of one arrangement, a sans serif typeface is part of another, and a serif font is a component in another. Consider styling these words differently using italicized versions and different weights and sizes of the fonts you select as well as all uppercase and uppercase and lowercase versions. Strive for the greatest amount of variety in these arrangements and stacking configurations. Print each arrangement as black type on white paper. Final size for each arrangement should be a 4- × 4-inch square. Mount all four arrangements on a single piece of black mount board with a 3-inch border.

Objectives

Practice selecting and arranging typefaces to create visually pleasing combinations.

Experiment with styling and sizing type in ways that create visual balance and harmony.

Develop familiarity by experimenting with a range of typefaces.

Become more skilled at working with fonts on the computer.

| imagery |

6

objectives

Appreciate the differences between photography and illustration.

Learn how photographs and illustration are used in a publication design.

Explore opportunities for cropping and using imagery creatively in a page layout.

Appreciate the differences between different illustration style and media.

Understand production issues as they relate to imagery.

introduction

As you've browsed through this book, you have probably noticed that each chapter opens with the combination of a chapter heading and an image. Editors, designers, and others involved in publication design understand that text alone is less likely to catch a reader's attention than text and an arresting image. Because "a picture is worth a thousand words," designers often use imagery to grab attention and establish an immediate connection with their audience. Marrying words with imagery is a powerful combination.

Because publication designers are often involved in selecting and commissioning imagery, it is important to understand the differences between the image options that are available as well as how to work most effectively with imagery in a layout.

IMAGERY

Photography

Because most people assume the camera never lies, photographs are generally regarded as the most credible type of imagery. This visual assumption sets up a situation in which the viewer is likely to accept a photograph as being real, without question—a premise that supports the visual power of photography. Photographs are often used in a photojournalistic way in support of newsworthy editorial or to document informative content. They are also used when accuracy or recognition is important. (See Figure 6-1).

We encounter photographs in practically everything we read. They catch our attention as cover imagery when we are browsing library and bookstore shelves or magazine stands.

They are typically used in catalogs where customers need to see realistic representations of products before they make a purchase decision. "What you see is what you get" is the assumption that consumers make when viewing photographs of merchandise. (See Figure 6-2).

Photography is also a powerful component in fashion and lifestyle magazines where they help readers visualize experiences they would like to recreate for themselves. Fashion magazine editors and art directors are well aware of this fact when they commission fashion photo shoots

Figure |6-1|

A photograph of the Osbournes assumes a dominant role in the opening spread of this *Vanity Fair* magazine article. The family's reputation for outrageousness, heightened in this photograph by Annie Leibovitz, and high recognition value were deciding factors in making this photograph the centerpiece of this layout. (Design by David Harris, Julie Weiss and Chris Mueller)

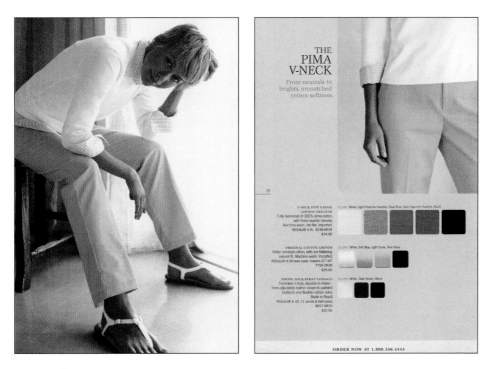

Figure |6-2|

Photographs are an important component in catalogs where they give consumers a realistic representation of what merchandise looks like. (*Lands Ends* catalog design by Laura O'Brien)

of models in exotic settings. Although it would be much easier and less expensive to shoot runway models or commission studio shots, they realize that their readers are more likely to make a positive connection with models in an exotic setting and envision themselves in similar fashions and circumstances. (See Figure 6-3).

The realism of photography also does a great job of stimulating interest and curiosity in any item or activity that suggests a pleasurable experience. A reader is far more likely to be drawn to a recipe when his or her appetite is stimulated by a photograph of an appetizing dish. Nothing does a better job of capturing every mouth-watering detail than a photograph. (See Figure 6-4).

Until recently, most photography was done traditionally with a camera and darkroom development. But digital cameras are increasingly being used because they bypass the photographic development process and can immediately be incorporated into computer-generated designs.

Because publication designers are frequently involved in commissioning photography and art-directing photographers, it is important to understand the different photographic processes available as well as the specialties and stylistic differences that exist from one photographer to the next. Designers typically look at the portfolios and get cost estimates before selecting and

Figure |6-3|

A Caribbean holiday is the setting for this fashion feature from *Details* magazine promoting leisure wear. (Magazine design by Dennis Freedman, Edward Leida, and Rockwell Harwood; photographs by Mikael Jansson)

Figure |6-4|

Appetite appeal is enhanced when readers see photographs of beautifully prepared desserts such as the ones featured in this article from *Real Simple* (Magazine design by Robert Valentine)

Choose the Right Photographic Option

Here is an overview of the different options from which to choose when finding, commissioning, or otherwise producing photographic imagery. Each imaging option has its own advantages and disadvantages.

- Slides and transparencies. *Pros:* Slides shot with a 35-mm camera and other transparencies offer excellent color reproduction because they offer greater tonal range than color photographic prints. A good quality transparency can be enlarged up to around seven times its size, or 700%. *Cons:* Slides and transparencies need to be scanned or digitized to be brought into computerized design and production.
- Digital photos. *Pros:* Digital photographs can quickly be incorporated into the digital production process. *Cons:* Image quality depends on the quality of the camera. Inexpensive digital cameras tend to produce unreliable results, particularly where detail and color are concerned.
- Photographic prints. *Pros:* Color and black-and-white prints can be easily examined and evaluated for quality. Because the tonal range in a print is already compressed, they are easier to match on press. *Cons:* Photographic prints cannot be enlarged much from their original size without losing clarity. They must be scanned or digitized to be brought into computerized design and production.

commissioning a photographer for a photo shoot. It is important to note that photo stylists, professionals who specialize in photographic arrangements, or hair and makeup professionals may also be involved in the cost of a photo shoot.

Judicious Cropping

When working with a photograph, your first impulse may be to use all of it, including the entire background. However, seasoned designers understand that removing portions of a photograph that detract or distract the viewer's attention from its central focus can draw attention to what is most meaningful about it. Knowing where and how to crop an image involves studying it and singling out its best part, including the portion that works best compositionally. (See Figure 6-5).

Determining how to crop an image often depends on the message that is being communicated. When working with photographs of an individual, there are times when the clothing and gesture or the surroundings of the subject may support the communication goal. Other times a close crop on an individual's face may be more appropriate, particularly if expression or emphasizing commonality among all humans is important. Interesting effects can also be achieved with creative cropping. (See Figure 6-6).

There may be occasions where a photograph's central image should be featured without any background at all. Isolating a subject from its background is called *outlining* or *silhouetting*. This technique may be your best or only option if the photograph is poorly composed or the background is so distracting that it needs to be entirely removed. This technique is frequently used when the shape of a silhouetted image works effectively as a compositional element in a layout. (See Figure 6-7).

(a)

(b)

Figure |6-5|

(a) The original photograph of the birds is not poorly composed, but can be improved. The birds with the most visual interest are in the photograph's center. (b) A vertical crop eliminates the photograph's slightly underexposed edges and yields a much more interesting image.

Figure |6-6|

(a) The original photograph shows a child engaged in an activity. (b) A closer crop eliminates distracting background elements and puts more emphasis on the face. (c) An even tighter crop focuses even more on features. Its unusual horizontal format adds visual interest. (d) A circular crop also focuses on features and suggests a sense of looking through a magnifying lens.

Illustration

The expressive quality of illustrations makes them valuable when a mood or feeling needs to be enhanced. A case in point is romance novels, which for years have depicted posed models on their covers as painted illustrations. That is because illustration is the more expressive of the two media.

The mood projected in an illustration is largely controlled and dictated by the illustration technique as well as the medium. Pen-and-ink, scratch board, pastel, gouache, and digital

Figure |6-7|

Isolating these binders from their background allows them to serve as compositional elements in these catalog layouts. As a result, interesting positive and negative spatial relationships occur. (Catalog design by Pattee Design)

Your Photograph Should Dictate Its Role in Your Design

Novice designers often try to make a photograph fit their composition. However, in practice, the opposite should happen—your composition should be dictated by the quality and size of your photograph. Follow these guidelines when working with photographs:

- Section off the best part of the photo. Use two L-shaped pieces of paper or card stock to help you determine the best part of the image and then determine how the design will best work with this cropped image.
- The quality of the photograph should determine its size, not the size of the area you have chosen for it in your design. Do not try to enlarge a photograph of marginal quality to make it fit your design.
- Great photographs with strong emotional or aesthetic appeal deserve first-class treatment. Give them the attention they deserve by giving them prominence in your layout.

drawing programs are just some of the media possibilities available. Each medium has a unique look and sensibility and, in the hands of different artists, can convey added nuance and feeling. Illustrators are often chosen based on the aesthetic sensibility of their style and how it supports the content and feeling of an article or book. (See Figure 6-8).

Illustrations are often used to enhance or exaggerate reality. Magazines frequently take advantage of this aspect in their depiction of celebrities and other personalities who are caricatured in ways that make their distinguishing characteristics more vivid. In the hands of a good illustrator, the results can be both humorous and entertaining. (See Figure 6-9).

In recent years, children's book illustration has emerged as a major market for illustrators. Picture books play a huge role in helping young children learn to read by reinforcing their understanding of the written word with imagery. Illustrations help engage young readers by providing a pictorial narrative that helps them understand a story on a visual level. Illustrations also help stimulate imagination and creativity by engaging young readers in explorations of fantasy.

Children's books feature a broad range of illustration styles and media. The degree of realism, color palette, and other elements incorporated in the illustrations are often a reflection of the book's audience's age level. (See Figure 6-10).

Illustrations can also help an audience visualize something that cannot be seen or better understand something that is complex. For instance, diagrammatic illustrations in instruction manuals help us assemble complex equipment. Artists' depiction of marine life and outer space, or medical illustrations in textbooks are all examples of ways that illustration is used to help us in our understanding of concepts that are difficult or impossible to photograph.

Illustrations, like photographs, are usually chosen or commissioned with output in mind. It is important to select or commission black-and-white media for output in black-and-white, rather than converting a color illustration to black and white.

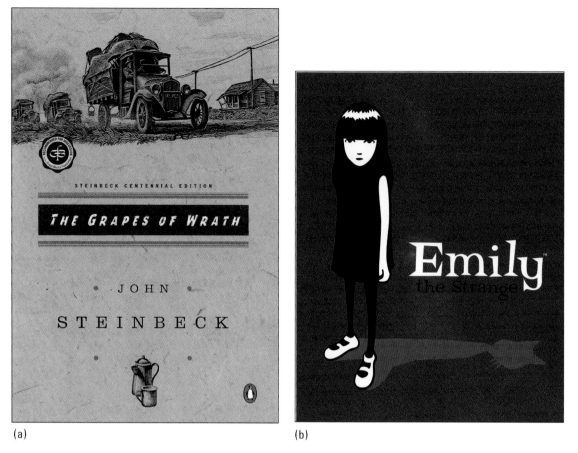

(a)   (b)

Figure |6-8|

Black-and-white illustration can include a range of media possibilities. Shown here are **(a)** a scratch board illustration (Book cover design by Paul Buckley), and **(b)** a digital rendering by Cosmic Debris for Chronicle Books.

Sources for Imagery

Some designers generate their own imagery, shooting pictures or creating drawings, paintings, or digital art for their page layouts. However, if you are not able to generate your own imagery, here are some resources commonly used:

- Royalty-free collections—Collections of illustrations and photographs can be purchased on CD-ROM as an inexpensive source of imagery. Their only drawback is that some of these images have a generic look. And, because they are available to anyone willing to purchase them, there is always the chance that an image from a royalty-free collection will appear (or may have already appeared) someplace else.
- Stock agencies—These agencies grant limited rights use of their photographs and illustrations for a fee. The drawbacks are similar to those for royalty-free collections in that there is no guarantee that an image has not or will not appear elsewhere. (See Figure 6-11).

(a)

(b)

Figure | 6-9 |

Caricature styles can vary greatly from one illustrator to the next. **(a)** Illustrator Al Hirschfeld was known for the economy of line that characterizes his distinctive pen-and-ink renderings. (Illustration of Joe DiMaggio for *Gentleman's Quarterly*). **(b)** Anita Kunz's illustration style recalls the detailed oil renderings of Renaissance artists. (Illustrations of Hollywood executives for *Premiere* magazine).

Image Terminology for Publication Production

Bringing an image into the design and production process requires digitizing or scanning it so that it can be printed in a way that will result in the best possible reproduction of the original. To determine the best way of scanning an image, it is important to know how prepress houses and scanning manufacturers classify imagery and the terminology they use.

- Continuous tone—A photograph or illustrated image that is comprised of a series of gray or color tones with gradations from one tone or color to the next, as opposed to color or tonal areas that are flat and distinct from one another.
- Grayscale—A continuous tone black-and-white image.
- Halftone—Reproducing a continuous-tone image by photographing it through a fine screen to convert the image into a series of dots. If it is a color image, it is called a CMYK halftone.
- Line art—Refers to a black-and-white image that does not have continuos tones such as a logo, a graphically reduced image, or a pen-and-ink illustration. Also called *bitmap*.

(a)

Figure |6-10|

Although they are used in books directed at elementary school-aged children, the illustration styles represented here are radically different. Tara Callahan King's illustration style **(a)** is much more exaggerated than that of Loren Long **(b)**.

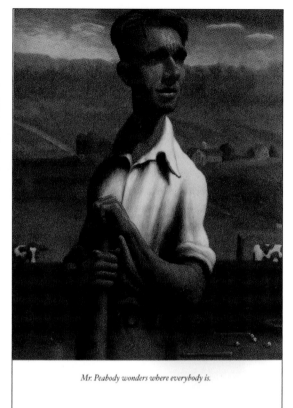

Mr. Peabody wonders where everybody is.

(b)

- Commissioned—Hiring a photographer or illustrator will yield a totally original piece of art. Professional photographs and illustrations will typically, but not always, cost more than stock or royalty-free collections.
- Found imagery—Small or flat objects such as leaves or coins can be directly scanned and incorporated into your designs. (See Figure 6-12).
- Uncredited illustrations and photographs found in printed materials at least 75 years old can be used. These images fall into a category called *public domain*, meaning that they are no longer protected by copyright.

Imagery as a Unifying Element

Throughout this book, the principles of unity and variety have been stressed. In Chapter Three you discovered how color can work as a unifying element in a publication and in Chapter Four how consistent typography can also add unity and variety. Chapter Five addressed the importance of a grid in establishing theme and variation. Imagery can serve a publication in the same way. The type of imagery that is featured and even the way it is handled can create a consistent look that helps to define a publication's personality. (See Figure 6-13). Consistent use of an illustration or photographic style can also help link a series of publications. (See Figure 6-14).

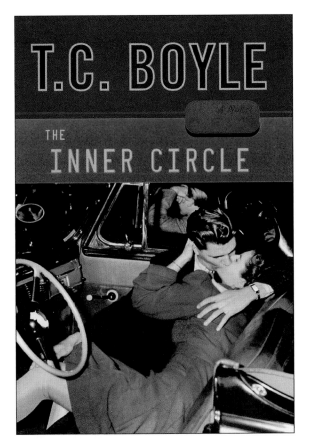

Figure | 6-11 |

The right to use the vintage photograph on this book cover was purchased from a stock agency that specializes in archival photography. (Cover design by Paul Buckley)

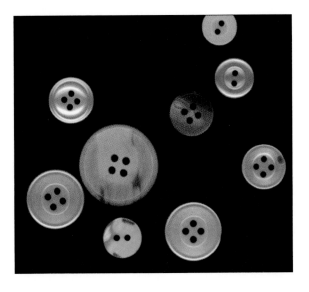

Figure | 6-12 |

Small, flat objects, such as the buttons shown here can be photographed by placing them on a scanner.

Figure |6-13|

The consistent use of small, black-and-white spot illustrations in *The New Yorker* helps unify the magazine and contributes to its sophisticated appeal.

Charts and Graphs

Nothing seems so boring and can alienate a reader more quickly than a page of statistics. That is where charts can help; they are more likely to engage a viewer's attention. They also help us visualize how the numbers look in a more meaningful and visually dynamic way.

Although there are many ways of plotting information or data, the types of charts that are most commonly used are pie charts, bar charts, and graphs. Pie charts demonstrate how a population segment or lump sum can be broken down into portions. They work well for showing how a group voted or how it is comprised in terms of demographic or opinion groups, how budget money was allocated, or where funds came from to arrive at a total. Pie charts do not necessarily

Figure | 6-14 |

The principles of theme and variation are at work in this series of covers for novels by author Graham Greene. The consistent illustration style and typography unify the series. The variation of subjects depicted and the changing colors add variety. (Cover designs by Paul Buckley; illustrations by Brian Cronin)

have to be plain circles or even pie shaped. For instance, designers sometimes take a photograph of a coin or currency and divide it into portions. (See Figure 6-15).

Bar charts work well for comparing data. Whether it is for sales or snow, bar charts show how things literally "stack up" when comparing what happened in one defined period of time with another. The bars in bar charts can run vertically or horizontally. They are often represented as stacks of coins, as pictograms, or as other symbols. (See Figure 6-16).

Graphs do a good job of plotting trends. They are particularly effective when showing dramatic growth or when comparing growth in several areas. They can be dressed up with pictorial representations or become eye-catching visual additions to a layout when color is applied to their lines. (See Figure 6-17).

Charts play an especially important role in annual reports, where financial information is plotted so that it can be more easily understood by readers. You will see more examples of the role charts play in an in-depth look at the design of an annual report in Chapter Eight: "Design Principles at Work".

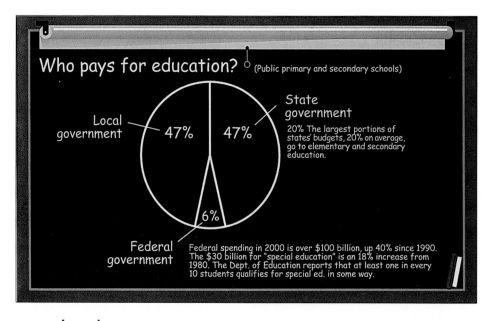

Figure | 6-15 |

Pie charts show how a total is a sum of its parts or how it can be broken down into portions.

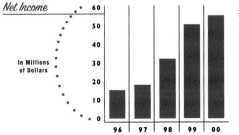

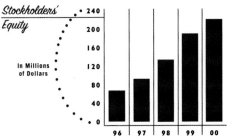

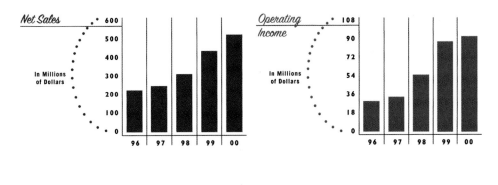

Figure | 6-16 |

Bar charts give a visual representation of how data stack up on a comparative basis. In this instance, a bar chart is used in an annual report to show an increase in stockholder's equity.

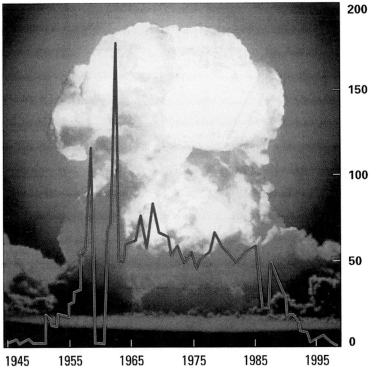

200

150

100

50

0

1945　　1955　　1965　　1975　　1985　　1995

Source: The Brookings Institution, 1998

Figure | 6-17 |

Graph charts help readers visualize trends.

SUMMARY

It is important to use photographs when recognition, documentation, and accuracy are crucial to the communication goal. There are many possibilities for commissioning photography and creative ways of cropping photographs. Illustration offers a range of looks and media possibilities, and can lend expressiveness to imagery. Illustration is used extensively in children's books for its ability to stimulate young readers and as a means of helping readers envision things that are imaginary or cannot be photographed. Photographs and illustrations can be created by the designer, commissioned, purchased, or licensed. Charts and graphs are a means of informative imagery and are used to make statistics more visually engaging and meaningful.

in review

1. Under what circumstances is it advantageous to use photography as opposed to illustration?

2. What is an outlined image? When can it be advantageous to use outlined imagery?

3. What can an illustration of a subject convey that a photograph cannot?

4. Why is illustration important to children's books?

5. What are the differences between a continuous tone and a halftone image?

6. What are the differences between pie charts, bar charts, and graphs, and how are they used?

projects

Project Title Cropping Photos

Project Brief Find a poorly composed photograph with no apparent focal point. This can be a snapshot or a photograph that you have purposely taken to fulfill this project. Make a photocopy of this photograph. Using two L-shaped pieces of cardboard to form a frame, find a focal point and determine where the photograph should be cropped to create an interesting and well-composed image. Mark off where the image should be cropped and trim to produce a finished image.

Objectives

Learn how to look at a photograph critically.

Practice using an L-shaped frame to find and isolate a photograph's best portion.

Project Title Creative Crops

Project Brief Search through magazines or other literature to find a full-body photograph of an individual. Make photocopies of this photograph or scan it and bring it into a photo-editing or other computer program that will enable you to crop the image. Create five new images of this individual by cropping the photograph in different ways. Limit your crops to rectangular and square formats. Experiment with crops that show gesture and ones that focus on facial features. Try to create interesting and well-composed final images that show a diverse range of viewpoints. Prepare your final images so they are approximately equivalent in size and mount them together in a pleasing arrangement on a single board.

Objectives

Experiment with cropping a photograph in a variety of ways.

Practice finding and isolating some of the best parts of a photograph.

Understand how cropping affects how a subject is perceived by a viewer.

Practice scaling images.

Improve composition skills by creating an arrangement of photographic images.

Project Title   Imagery as a Unifier

Project Brief   Find a magazine or a piece of literature, other than a book, that features illustration prominently and consistently throughout. Analyze what the image treatment is and how it is being used to help unify the publication by asking yourself the following questions:

- Are the images illustrations or photographs?

- What stylistic technique is being used that gives them visual consistency?

- Are the images cropped in a consistent manner?

- What other attributes are contributing to a consistent look?

Objectives

Understand how consistent image treatment can act as a unifying element.

Learn how to recognize stylistic consistency and various stylistic techniques.

Recognize when a consistent cropping technique serves as a unifying element.

notes

| the publication in the third dimension |

objectives

Appreciate the importance of format in publication design.

Understand how size and color can support a publication's communication goal.

Appreciate the roles that paper and binding play in a publication's design and format.

Study unusual formats that go beyond traditional perceptions of publication design.

Know the role that a cover plays in a publication's design.

Understand how content is organized to aid reader navigation.

introduction

Unlike posters, ads, or other two-dimensional designs, publications have form, volume, and weight. Like any other three-dimensional object, a publication occupies space and can be viewed from its front, back, and sides.

Publications also have an exterior and an interior. A publication's exterior, its front and back covers and spine, could be viewed much like packaging—it protects and projects what the reading experience will be.

A publication's interior pages are where content is delivered. Although the design of each page in a publication is important, how well those pages work together to create organization and continuity is equally as important. The sequencing of information and multidimensional aspects of publication design present designers with unique challenges.

This chapter discusses how to arrive upon an appropriate format for a publication and discover creative ways to exploit the three-dimensional potential in a publication by examining examples of such designs. You will also learn about the role a cover plays in a publication's design. Because paper and binding are important factors in publication design, you will be introduced to different binding methods and learn about how paper can impact a publication's size and appearance. Finally, you will learn about the importance of establishing rhythm and points of entry in a publication.

Format Follows Function

In Chapter Two you learned about the importance of format. Making an informed decision on a publication's size and portability relative to its communication goal is an important first step in a publication's design.

Size and Color

This textbook serves as a good case in point. Its 8- × 10-inch format was chosen because this size works best for presenting and showcasing its content. As a point of comparison, let us examine how an alternative format might have worked:

Imagine how different this book would look and feel if it was cut in half and had twice as many pages. As the reader, you would be viewing and absorbing the same amount of content, but your perception of it would be very different when experienced within the context of this alternative format. A book twice as thick might give the impression of having lots to read. This feature might draw the type of reader who would be inclined to pick up a publication full of literary content, such as *Reader's Digest*, but it could likely alienate design students who are typically visual learners, as well as others wanting information in a "quick read." A format half this size would require showing the visual examples in this book at a smaller scale, a factor that would probably inhibit a full understanding of the design principles that are presented and explored because it would be harder to view the details in these examples.

This textbook also features four-color printing—crucial to full-color reproduction and an understanding of how color works in the examples and design principles that are discussed. Printing a book in four colors is typically more complicated and expensive than printing one or two colors. A text-heavy book such as a novel would not warrant the additional expense involved in four-color printing. However, it is a necessary expense for this book in which full-color reproduction of visuals plays an important role in supporting content. Imagine how differently this book would function if the presentation of visual material was confined to just one or two colors!

In addition to choosing a format that supports this textbook's content within its interior pages, this book's designer also considered how its format and cover would function in book stores and other environments where its retail presence must compete with other books of this type. A textbook with a half-size cover and limited color might not be as likely to attract and engage its audience of beginning designers. This book's cover, at its present size and in full color, is more likely to catch the attention of interested readers.

In addition to its vertical and horizontal dimensions, a publication also has volume and thickness. A publication's thickness or bulk is obviously related to the number of pages it contains. A book with 16 pages will appear to have less bulk than one that contains 60 pages. A publication that appears to have many pages sends a message to prospective readers that it contains lots of information. On the other hand, one that appears thin will send the opposite message.

When considering the format of any publication, it is important to determine whether a publication's audience will respond favorably to the idea of being presented with lots of information or if they would be more responsive to a publication that contains a small amount of information.

A publication's dimensions, its thickness, and its width and height should support its communication goal. Making this determination is an important first-step in the design of any publication. (See Figure 7-1).

Paper

Publication designers can control a viewer's perception of the number of pages a publication contains by selecting paper that adds to or reduces a publication's bulk. Papers come in varying degrees of thickness and, because the thickness of a paper also affects its weight, both aspects are described by the term *basis weight*. A paper with a high basis weight adds bulk to a publication, whereas one with a low basis weight reduces bulk. In some cases, practicality leads to the selection of a thin paper with a low basis weight, such as for bibles and dictionaries that contain hundreds of pages.

Other times, it is important to send a message that a publication is packed with content. In these instances, publication designers create the illusion of more pages than a publication actually contains by selecting a paper with a high basis weight to add bulk. Understanding how a paper's basis weight can affect the bulk and weight of a publication is an important aspect of publication design. (See Figure 7-2). It is so important that designers typically make

Figure |7-1|

Although at first glance it looks like a printed box, this catalog of stock imagery is a book with printing on the edge of its pages. Unlike most catalogs of this type that feature many images on a page, the small size of this catalog (3½ × 3⅝ inches) allowed for just one or two images per page. The result is a catalog with considerably more pages than most, giving it a thick, chunky presence. (Font Shop catalog design by Stefan Sagmeister, Matthias Ernstberger, Sagmeister, Inc.)

a *bulking dummy* or request one from a paper merchant before they begin the design process in order to see and experience how a publication will look and feel with the dimensions, number of pages, and the paper they have chosen.

The texture or surface characteristics of a paper and the perception of quality a paper projects are also important factors in publication design. When you compare the inexpensive paper used for printing newspaper to the premium coated paper used for a fashion magazine, there is an obvious difference in the way these papers look and feel. There is also an appreciable difference in their ability to reproduce printed type and imagery. Newsprint paper tends to absorb ink and makes images and type appear fuzzier when compared to the crisp reproduction capabilities of a premium printing paper.

Printing papers come in a wide range of colors, surface textures, and basis weights. Papers with subtle patterns, fiber inclusions, and varying degrees of translucency can also add textural richness and aesthetic appeal to a publication's design. Any designer wanting to get involved in publication design should have a basic understanding of the different categories and varieties of paper and how they perform on press. Paper can play an important role in defining a publication's personality and achieving its communication goal, and can be used in many creative ways to support a concept. (See Figure 7-3).

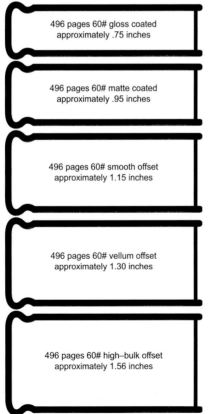

496 pages 60# gloss coated
approximately .75 inches

496 pages 60# matte coated
approximately .95 inches

496 pages 60# smooth offset
approximately 1.15 inches

496 pages 60# vellum offset
approximately 1.30 inches

496 pages 60# high–bulk offset
approximately 1.56 inches

Figure |7-2|

This diagram demonstrates how papers with varying basis weights can affect the bulk or thickness of a publication.

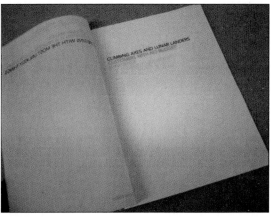

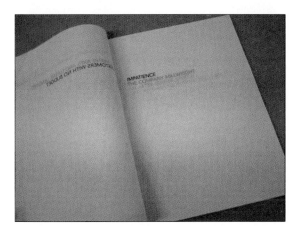

Figure |7-3|

The opening message of this annual report for Herman Miller gradually reveals itself as pages are turned. Printing its cover and pages on layers of translucent vellum made this effect possible by allowing part of the message to be visible, while other parts remain barely discernible. (Annual report design by BBK Studio)

Binding

Binding is also an important consideration in a publication's design. Binding options are affected, to some extent, by a publication's bulk. Some types of binding require a minimum number of pages, whereas others will not work for a publication with a large number of pages.

Binding can also affect a publication's ability to function in a way that supports its goal. A cookbook or reference manual, for instance, will likely better serve its reader if it can lie open flat so that its pages can be viewed while hands are free to do other things. Binding options such as case binding, ring binders, lie-flat perfect binding, double-loop wire, and spiral binding allow a book to lay flat open. (See Figure 7-4).

Another consideration to keep in mind when looking at binding options is the visibility of the spine—an important factor if a publication needs to be identified by its spine on a bookshelf. Cost and production considerations also come into play when selecting binding. Some binding methods, such as case binding, can have a lower cost per item for large quantities, but

Figure |7-4|

Certain types of binding, such as the comb binding on this cookbook, allow a book to lay open flat so that it can be consulted while hands are busy with food preparation. (Illustrations by Debby Mumm)

become cost-prohibitive for small quantities because of the set-up time involved. Certain types of binding are more durable than others and should be used for books and other publications intended for long-term use. Some binding methods cause *cross overs* (type and imagery that crosses over in a spread from one page to the next) to get lost in the gutter. Publication designers generally choose a binding for a publication with utility, cost, and a publication's overall design in mind. (See Figure 7-5).

Alternative Formats

What defines a publication? Does it have to consist of bound pages? Some of the most impressive and memorable designs go beyond conventional perceptions of what a publication should

Perfect Binding

Case Binding

Saddle Stitch Binding

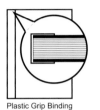

Plastic Grip Binding

Plastic Comb Binding

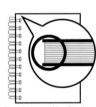

Sprial Wire Binding

Double-Loop Wire Binding

Figure |7-5|

There are many binding options. Although a printer or bindery can usually offer advice on what type of binding is best, it is important to have a general knowledge of the advantages and disadvantages of each type.

be. It could be argued that publications are printed, time-based media, in that the viewer is led from beginning to end through a sequence of pages. Therefore, a publication's binding and format are at the discretion of the designer and others involved in a publication's design. (See Figure 7-6).

Children's books frequently take advantage of unusual materials and formats to create visual surprises. Pop-up images, books that mimic toys, and other aspects that encourage touching or manipulation are often more likely to engage children than conventional books by inviting interactivity. (See Figure 7-7).

Covers and Spine

A publication's covers and spine contain and protect its interior pages as well as identify its content for potential readers. A cover should also hint at what the reading experience is like by expressing the personality or voice behind the publication. How this is achieved and how

Figure |7-6|

This self-promotional brochure for BBK Studio presents the credentials for each of its 12 employees on 2- × 3-inch cards. The 12 employee cards and a cover card, entitled "analog studio tour," are connected by a hinged vinyl sleeve that is accordion folded so that the cards fit neatly into the metal case. When the recipient opens the case, the concept of the studio tour is supported by seeing the cards in sequence, as though meeting each of the employees, one by one, on an actual visit. (Design by BBK Studio)

a cover is designed to support these aspects is largely a result of the venue or circumstances in which the publication will first be seen. There are major differences between how a publication is experienced when it is first encountered in a retail environment versus nonretail venues, such as receiving it in the mail.

Covers in the Retail Environment

Magazine and book covers are designed with the knowledge that they are competing for a consumer's attention among many other publications. For publications that appear in a bookstore or magazine rack, it is important to design a cover that functions much like a point-of-purchase display. Book covers are often designed as though they are mini posters, combining words with attention-grabbing imagery to catch a potential reader's attention and convey some sense of what the reading experience will be. (See Figure 7-8).

Magazine covers are like mini ads. They typically include imagery that will attract and draw potential readers, but they also try to communicate as much as possible about a magazine's content and personality. Attitude is established with typography, color, and the style and treatment of imagery that is used. Cover lines hint at lots of great reading in the pages within. A magazine's logo and important information is typically placed at the top of the cover so that it is immediately visible in a magazine rack. The designer's challenge is often in arranging

Figure |7-7|

Books that appear to be toys, such as this one depicting a castle, are sometimes more likely to attract young children than those with a more traditional format. (Book design by Peter Lippman)

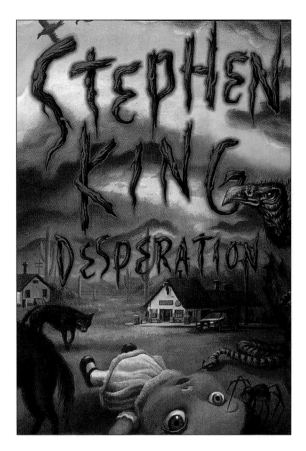

Figure |7-8|

A reading experience of mystery and horror is clearly conveyed in this cover design for a Stephen King novel. The illustration communicates aspects of the story, such as its desolate Southwest setting, while its typography supports a sense of the macabre. (Cover design by Paul Buckley; illustration and typography by Mark Ryden)

cover line text so that information is presented clearly and forcefully, but in a way that is balanced and does not overwhelm a magazine's logo and cover image. (See Figure 7-9).

Nonretail Covers

Some magazines are primarily subscription based. Although there may be some overlap in terms of retail

Figure |7-9|

Cover lines and celebrity photos play a prominent role in this cover design of *Premiere* magazine. In this example, outlining the cover's image helps provide flexibility, allowing heads to be superimposed on the magazine's logo without losing legibility. Cover lines assume prominence according to their hierarchy and are visually separated from each other by their size, color, placement, and different background treatment. Switching styles and weights of typography also helps create visual interest and contrast in the cover lines. (Magazine design by Dirk Barnett, photography by Norman Jean Ray)

Figure |7-10|

CMYK is a primarily subscription-based magazine that recognizes student excellence in the communication arts. Because its revenue is not dependent on retail sales, cover lines are not an important component in its cover designs. (Magazine design by Genevieve Astrelli and Amy Chong)

sales, magazines that receive most of their revenue from subscriptions are not as concerned with establishing an in-store presence. Subscribers have already made a decision to purchase the magazine. The covers of these magazines are typically more subtle and not as driven by content-promoting cover lines. (See Figure 7-10).

Catalogs and annual report covers are similar. Because these publications are freely distributed, there is less need to promote content with fewer lines on the cover. In these instances, a cover communicates and supports the image and mission of the company or organization it represents, as well as the publication's goal. As part of a concept-driven approach, the cover can create a sense of mystery, piquing interest in a reader, and delivering a surprise within. (See Figure 7-11).

Navigating Content

Publications with a story to tell, such as novels, comic books and children's books, have a predetermined organization. The plot leads and guides the viewer through a logical sequence of pages from beginning to end. However, the organization of other types of literature is often based on what is most likely to hook and engage prospective readers. To some extent, hierarchy and order is determined by attracting and piquing interest.

For example, an effective magazine cover contains written and visual information that attracts and entices a potential reader. After the reader opens the magazine, the table of contents acts

Figure |7-11|

The cover of this college catalog for California College of Arts and Crafts (now called California College of the Arts) intrigues with its mysterious "CCAC" against a backdrop of the sky. Its subtlety sets the reader up for a surprise when the cover is turned and finds interior pages filled with "in-your-face" large-scale type and imagery. (Catalog design by Vanderbyl Design)

much like a menu, giving the reader a taste of what the reading experience will be. From there, editorial content is typically organized so that information that is quick to read is positioned near the front of the publication. The idea is to hook potential readers with content that is both meaningful and an "easy read." The core of the magazine contains more in-depth content within its *feature section*.

Points of Entry

The reader is accustomed to using the table of contents to find specific editorial content. However, a reader may become drawn to an editorial item without initially intending to read it. If you thumb through any publication, powerful imagery, strong color, and large, contrasting type are likely to catch your eye as they stand out in a sea of text. These items and graphic treatments that draw a reader's attention to items on a page, such as pull quotes, subheads, and sidebars, are called *points of entry*.

Points of entry are visual clues. They help readers by calling their attention to items of interest as they randomly thumb through a publication's pages. In addition to drawing the reader's attention to an item on a page or spread, they can also serve in a broader context by helping a reader navigate through a publication. In this book, for instance, the imagery and bold typography that are incorporated into the design of each chapter's opening pages serve as points of entry.

When considering points of entry and what readers see first, it is important to note that items positioned on right-hand pages and closest to the edge of a page are more likely to be noticed first. Magazines are aware of this visibility factor and typically place fractional ads (those smaller than a full page) on the outside edge of a page, rather than close to the gutter. Many magazines also charge a higher rate for ads placed on a right-hand page.

Establishing Rhythm and Balance

In Chapter Five you learned how typographic techniques can break up large bodies of text and add visual interest and organization to a page. Visual points of entry scattered thoughout a publication, such as large photographs or bold graphic effects, act in much the same way. They stand out in contrast against pages that have large areas of text and little or no visual activity. Although visual points of entry should be established with the idea of supporting content and guiding a reader through a publication, it is also important to keep visual balance in mind when determining where high-impact visual material will occur. Those pages need to be balanced by "quiet" pages that contain little visual activity. (See Figure 7-12).

SUMMARY

A publication's design begins with determining its format: its width, height, thickness, and amount of color involved. Format should support a publication's content and its goal. The perception of the amount of content a publication contains is influenced by its bulk or thickness, a factor that is influenced by the basis weight of the paper on which it is printed. The quality of a paper, its surface characteristics, and color also have an impact on a publication's design and how it is perceived. There are many types of binding available, each with its own distinct advantages and disadvantages. Binding should be chosen with utility, cost, and aesthetic appeal in mind. Some of the most impressive publication designs go beyond traditional definitions and formats. Covers play an important role in a retail environment where the publication is in competition for a reader's attention. In a nonretail environment, covers can play a more subtle role in a concept-driven design

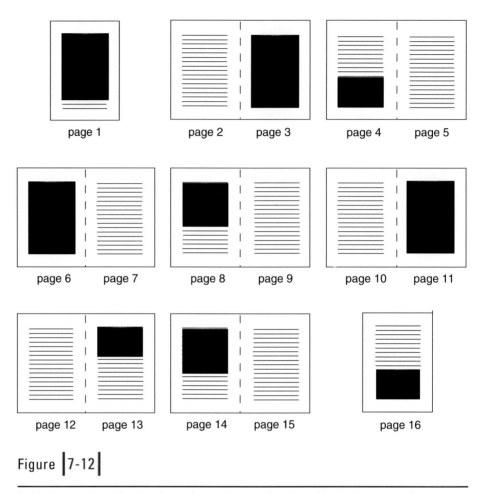

Figure |7-12|

In this diagram of a publication's layout, image placement is indicated by the black rectangles. Notice how a sense of rhythm is established by alternating pages with lots of visual activity with those that have very little.

approach. Readers are typically drawn into a publication and navigate it by looking for points of entry—visual clues that catch their attention and direct their eye to items of interest. A well-designed publication balances pages containing lots of visual activity with text-heavy pages.

in review

1. Why are color and size important considerations in a publication's design?

2. How does paper impact a publication's design?

3. What does the term "basis weight" mean?

4. What is a bulking dummy and why is it important in a publication's design?

5. What aspects should be considered when choosing binding?

6. How do covers in the retail environment differ from nonretail covers?

7. What are points of entry and how are they used in a publication?

8. How can rhythm and balance be achieved within a publication?

projects

Project Title Make a Bulking Dummy

Project Brief Create a 24-page bulking dummy by assembling six sheets of office bond (photocopier) paper folded in half and stapled in the middle. You will have a 5½- × 8½-inch booklet that should have a thickness of about one sixteenth of an inch. From there, create another bulking dummy the same size and with the same number of pages using six sheets of 8½- × 11-inch paper that, when folded, will allow you to create a booklet with a thickness of approximately one fourth of an inch. Browse through papers at an art supply store or other sources to find paper that is thick enough to fulfill the assignment. All 24 pages must be the same type of paper. This second booklet will likely be too thick to allow the sheets to be stapled together. Instead, use paper fasteners or another means of securing them.

Objectives

Understand how paper can affect the bulk of a publication.

Become aware of the variety of possibilities paper can offer.

Practice making a publication dummy.

Project Title Binding Questions and Answers

Project Brief Find an example of a publication that demonstrates each of the following types of binding:

- Case bound

- Perfect bound

- Saddle stitch

- Spiral or double-loop wire

Answer the following questions for each example:

- What is the purchase price of the publication?

- How thick is it?

- How many pages does it contain?

- Is there a printed spine?

- Does type or imagery get lost in the gutter when it crosses over a spread?

- Can the publication be opened to lie flat?

- How durable does the binding appear to be?

Objectives

Learn how to recognize different types of binding.

Understand the role that binding plays in a publication's design and purpose.

notes

THE LITTLE FRIEND

a novel by the author of THE SECRET HISTORY

DONNA TARTT

| design principles at work |

8

objectives

Find out how design elements and principles discussed in earlier chapters are applied to examples of award-winning design.

Understand how a publication's communication goals and audience affect its design.

Learn about the differences between magazine, newspaper, book, annual report, and promotional brochure design.

Find out how content and purpose drive the design of magazines, newspapers, books, annual reports, and promotional brochures.

introduction

Within each chapter of this book, you learned how a specific design principle or element was applied to a variety of publications. You may have seen an example in Chapter Four that demonstrated how typography was used in support of that publication's design, but wondered what role imagery and color played in the overall success of that publication's design.

This chapter dissects six publications, each an example of one of the following: a magazine, newspaper, newsletter, book, annual report, and promotional brochure. With each example, you will learn how all of the design principles and elements discussed in this book have worked together to produce a successful design. You will also learn about the design challenges that are unique to each of these types of publications.

Magazines

Magazines are broadly defined as *periodicals* in that they are published with regularity on an ongoing basis. Magazines are generally produced and distributed on a weekly, biweekly, monthly, bimonthly, or quarterly basis.

Unlike newspapers and other design vehicles that reach a broad audience, magazines are frequently directed to a narrow demographic. A magazine's audience may be age or gender specific. For instance, magazines such as *Gentlemen's Quarterly* and *Esquire* are targeted to young men, whereas *Cosmopolitan* and *Elle* are directed at young women. These magazines have editorial content specific to and a look that reflects the lifestyle of its audience. Other magazines exist to serve special interests or trades.

In addition to front and back covers, features that most magazines have in common include a table of contents, masthead, departments and columns, and a feature section. In addition to these editorial items, most magazines also have advertising.

The table of contents appears toward the front of the magazine and is followed by the magazine's *masthead*, a listing of staff members, copyright information, and the editorial office address and telephone number. Departments and columns are typically positioned in the front and in the back of a magazine. These editorial features are usually short and often limited in visual material so that they do not compete with advertising. (Examples common to many magazines are letters from readers and an editor's column). A magazine's feature section is generally at its core. This is where more lengthy editorial content appears, such as articles and photo essays. Because this section is less likely to be interrupted by ads, publication designers typically have more creative freedom in their design of feature section articles.

Example: *HOW* magazine

HOW magazine is an important resource for designers, offering useful information as well as examples of award-winning design. Because the magazine helps graphic designers stay on top of current design trends, it is essential for this trade journal to be as well-designed and up-to-date as the design and designers it celebrates.

Its current design was developed by Pentagram's DJ Stout and Erin Mayes. Stout and Mayes wanted the design to reflect the magazine's personality, which Stout characterizes as "friendly and accessible." Stout describes *HOW* as "supportive and inspiring, like a good coach or influential mentor." The magazine's design projects a casual, yet friendly tone and incorporates graphic elements that suggest design process to support the magazine's instructional aspects.

Newspapers

Unlike magazines, which often target narrow audiences, newspapers give information to a broad range of readers. They give people time-sensitive information on a daily basis and are

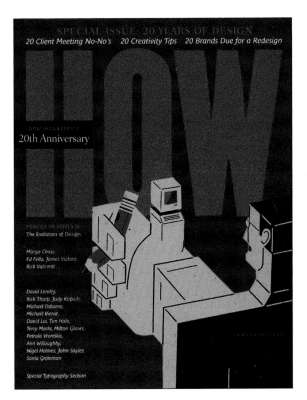

Figure |8-1|

Cover design of *HOW* magazine is based on rendering its logo in a way that thematically links it with the focus of each issue. In this example, it becomes part of the background in an illustration by David Plunkert. Collaborating with a creative professional in the design of each issue's cover is an important aspect of the magazine's cover design. The 20th Anniversary banner is cleverly incorporated into the logo as part of the letter "H."

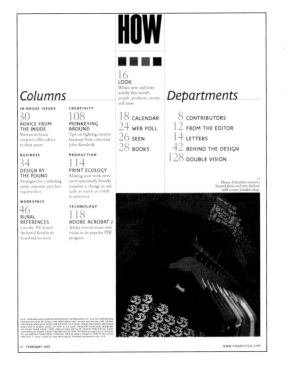

Figure |8-2|

The table of contents establishes a look that is carried throughout the magazine. Some of the attributes established here include a five-column grid, plenty of white space, and four squares representing the four process colors: cyan, magenta, yellow, and black.

Figure |8-3|

The masthead for *HOW* appears on the same page where contributors' photographs and biographies are featured. Because contributors' photographs are both black-and-white and color, the magazine's design staff reworks them in a photo-editing program for a consistent look.

designed with the idea that they will be read and then thrown away. Because they have such a short shelf life, newspapers do not need a protective cover or binding. They are also produced as cheaply as possible, typically printed with minimal color on inexpensive, newsprint paper. Newspapers do not strive to project a high-quality image, but they do need to communicate a sense of stability and reliability while simultaneously engaging and entertaining their readers.

Because there is no time to labor over organizing content, newspapers usually do not have a table of contents to direct readers to editorial content. They are structured in a way that breaks down editorial content into sections—a series of pages that are folded together. The most newsworthy items appear in the first section of the paper. The expression "front page news" is fitting in that content that is most important will appear on a newspaper's front page. The first section with the most newsworthy content is wrapped around the other sections of the paper. Regional papers generally break down their content into sections that focus on local news, sports, business, lifestyle content, and classified advertising. Larger ads, called *display ads*, are interspersed among editorial content.

Because of their large format, most newspapers are typically structured with grid format that can be broken down into six to eight columns. Pages are typically divided horizontally as well as vertically so that stories become components in the make up of a page. Because headlines

Figure | 8-4 |

Airy layouts with lots of white space help differentiate the editorial pages of *HOW* from color-heavy advertising. The magazine's design also uses lots of outlined imagery, a feature that also helps "open up" its pages.

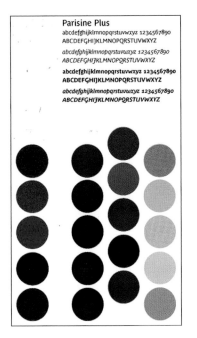

Figure | 8-5 |

HOW magazine's headline typeface projects personality without sacrificing legibility. To support the magazine's mission of providing design and production information, the magazine's color palette emphasizes the four process colors.

(a)

(b)

Figure |8-6|

The use of outlined imagery and flexible, five-column grid allow for playful, creative layouts. Typographic emphasis is established by strategic placement and the use of bright, contrasting color.

are often read at a glance, and newspapers need to be read quickly, legible typography is extremely important to newspaper type.

Because newspapers have no cover, the headlines on a newspaper's front page generally sell the paper. Creating proper balance and hierarchy between a newspaper's front-page headline typography and its photography is critical. Newspapers tend to be text heavy and need to communicate lots of information within a limited area. Typographic hierarchy is created by varying the scale and weight of the type.

Example: The Miami Herald

Residents of greater Miami, Florida, have looked to *The Miami Herald* as their primary source for printed news since its first issue was published in 1903. More than 100 years later, the design of this venerable publication sets the standard among regional newspapers for its reader-friendly format. Its designer, Mario Garcia of Garcia Media, incorporated navigational aids and other graphic devices into the design to create visual points of entry and to help organize content for readers wanting information in a hurry. Garcia developed these features to accommodate younger readers whom he characterizes as "supersonic readers," those who scan a paper much like scanning a Web page, by skimming for information they need and ignoring the rest.

Newsletters

Newsletters are often thought of as "stepchildren" of newspapers and magazines. They are similar in that they are issued on a regular basis, and contain articles. They also may incorporate other features seen in magazines and newspapers such as departments, columns, and advertising and be designed and formatted in ways that are similar to a newspaper or magazine. The difference is that newsletters exist on a much smaller scale than magazines or newspapers. They have fewer pages, narrower distribution, and usually much smaller budgets than newspapers or magazines. Because they need to be produced inexpensively, they are typically printed in one or two colors and have limited photography.

Newsletters tend to project an image that gives readers a sense that they are reading something that is not being produced on a grand scale, an aspect that makes this format a logical choice for employee news, community information, clubs, and other situations wherein readers want to feel as though they are part of a small, intimate, cohesive group.

Example: *Why*

At first glance, *Why* may appear to be a magazine, but it is actually a company newsletter for Fidelity Investments. Its designer, Clifford Stoltze of Stoltze Design, chose to emulate the look and feel of a magazine to support an editorial approach that would devote each issue to

Figure | 8-7 |

The front page of the *The Miami Herald* features a navigation bar at the far left that lets readers get an overview of each issue's highlights. Readers are directed to the section of the paper where each story appears.

Figure | 8-8 |

Many of *The Miami Herald* newspaper's feature stories contain a "Smart Box," a navigational aid that directs readers to supplementary information and relevant details.

Figure | 8-9 |

A special section of the paper, the "5 minute herald," accommodates readers who like to skim by letting them read briefs of each section's top stories. This section functions much like a "mini newspaper" within the paper.

Figure |8-10|

No matter how important or relevant the news, a newspaper crammed with text can often alienate readers. *The Miami Herald* takes this into consideration with its "Tropical Life" section, which seems more like a magazine with its prominent cover image and half-size format.

Figure | 8-11 |

Figure | 8-11 |

Although *The Miami Herald* uses the same combination of fonts in its design, type is styled differently to help the reader differentiate between news features and editorial columns. Italicized headlines and an initial cap signal to readers that they are reading opinion rather than news.

a division of the company. This in-depth, focused approach was so similar to what a magazine might do with its feature section that the format made sense, even though each issue is just 6 to 12 pages.

The mission of *Why* is to show why employees and their activities are important to Fidelity's well being. The contemporary look of its logo and other aspects of the design were created with its target audience in mind, a youthful group of primarily 25- to 35-year-old employees.

Figure |8-12|

The *Why* logo and headline typography project an edgy sensibility that establishes an immediate connection with youthful employees. This issue's focus on working under pressure is heightened by the emotional connotations associated with the color red.

Figure |8-13|

Strong typography and pull quotes, set with red vertical rules, help break up text in this article layout. Close cropping of photographs of workers puts the focus on human interaction.

Figure | 8-14 |

Digital layering and photomanipulation give photographs of employees a sense of blurred action and people working quickly and efficiently under deadline pressure. The technique also added a contemporary look and visual interest to traditional imagery.

Book Design

Book design typically places the emphasis on the cover or jacket design. As discussed in Chapter Seven, book covers present a design challenge in that they must communicate in an instant what the reading experience is like. The designer of a book's cover or jacket must be totally familiar with the book and have enough insight into its character and purpose to communicate this in its cover. After reading a book, its cover designer will develop a design concept. Concepts may be image based and incorporate illustration or photography or they may be typographically driven. Other publishing professionals such as the book's editor or author may get involved in the design process as well. Book covers typically include the book's title, author's name, and sometimes supplementary information. The book cover's designer must design the typography for all of these items and then incorporate an image into the design, if an image is part of the concept.

Although a book's cover or jacket plays an important role in attracting a reader and drawing their interest, the layout of a book also must support the book's content and purpose. The pages that follow the cover need to engage a reader and lead them further into the book. Books usually start with a title page, which includes the author's byline and followed by or facing a copyright page that lists copyright information, ISBN number, the publisher's address, and other information the publisher is legally obligated to print. Dedications and acknowledgments follow. If the book is divided into chapters, the table of contents is next in sequence followed by a prologue, forward, or introduction.

Books vary widely in the amount of imagery they include. They can be pictorial essays focusing solely on the work of an artist or photographer, or they may contain nothing but text. However, the one attribute that the interior of most well-designed books have in common is attention to detail and typography. Because books (particularly if they are hard-cover, case bound) have a long life, book publishing professionals are acutely aware of the importance of perfecting every detail of a book. For those involved in its interior design, a balanced layout and elegant typography are critical, as is designing with ease of reading in mind.

Example: *The Little Friend*

Designing a book jacket for *The Little Friend*, a mystery novel by Donna Tartt, presented designer Chip Kidd with several challenges. The tremendous success of Tartt's first novel required a cover concept that promoted the author while simultaneously communicating to potential readers a sense of the novel's theme. Kidd also needed to convey the dark nature of

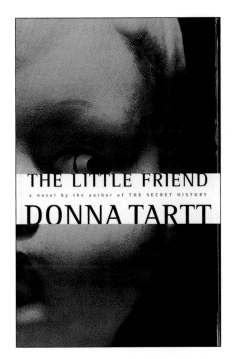

Figure |8-15|

Geoff Spear's photograph makes the most of the mannequin's worried look. The book's title and author's name appear against a white background as though the photograph of the mannequin, with its eye on the text, is closing in on it.

ABCDEabcde12345

Figure |8-16|

Chip Kidd's choice of typography for the title of the book also makes readers feel uneasy. The typeface Rotis resembles a serif font, but the absence of brackets at the bottom of the letterforms gives readers an unsettling feeling that something is missing.

Figure |8-17|

The mannequin image wraps around the book's spine and appears on the back cover as well as the front.

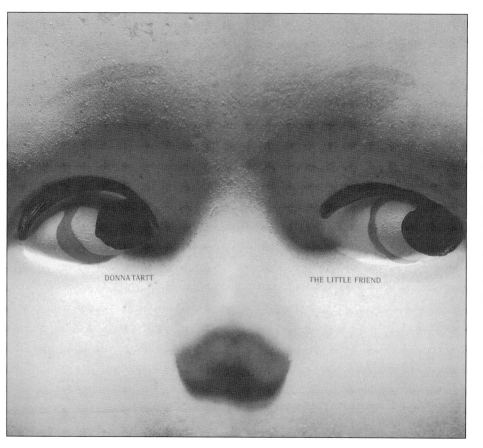

Figure |8-18|

When the book is opened, the cover image appears again. Instead of a title page, designer Chip Kidd chose to create a spread for the title and author's byline, cropping in on the mannequin's eyes to serve as a backdrop. When readers open the book, they get the sense that they can never escape the watchful eyes of the worried mannequin.

Prologue.

Are you sure? she said to Allison. Did the kitty scratch you?

Allison shook her head no. Charlotte knelt and checked her over quickly; no bumps, no bruises. The cat had disappeared.

Still uneasy, Charlotte kissed Allison on the forehead and led her into the house ("Why don't you go see what Ida's doing in the kitchen, honey?") and then went back out for the baby. She had felt these dreamlike flashes of panic before, usually in the middle of the night and always when a child was less than six months old, bolting upright from a sound sleep to rush to the crib. But Allison wasn't hurt, and the baby was fine. . . . She went into the living room and deposited Harriet with her aunt Adelaide, picked up the napkins on the dining-room rug, and—still half-sleepwalking, she didn't know why—trailed into the kitchen to get the baby's jar of apricots.

Her husband, Dix, had said not to wait supper. He was out duck-hunting. That was fine. When Dix wasn't at the bank, he was usually out hunting or over at his mother's house. She pushed open the kitchen doors and dragged a stool over to get the baby's apricots from the cabinet. Ida Rhew was bending low, pulling a pan of rolls from the oven. *God*, sang a cracking Negro voice from the transistor radio. *God don't never change.*

That gospel program. It was something that haunted Charlotte, though she'd never mentioned it to anyone. If Ida hadn't had that racket turned up so loud they might have heard what was going on in the yard, might have known that something was wrong. But then (tossing in her bed at night, trying restlessly to trace events to a possible First Cause) it was she who had made pious Ida work on Sunday in the first place. *Remember the Sabbath and keep it holy.* Jehovah in the Old Testament was always smiting people down for far less.

These rolls are nearly done, Ida Rhew said, stooping to the oven again.

Ida, I'll get those. I think it's about to rain. Why don't you bring the clothes in and call Robin to supper.

When Ida—grouchy and stiff—creaked back in with an armload of white shirts, she said: He won't come.

You tell him to get in here this minute.

I don't know where he is. I done called half a dozen times.

Maybe he's across the street.

Ida dropped the shirts in the ironing basket. The screen door banged shut. *Robin,* Charlotte heard her yell. *You come on, or I'll switch your legs.*

And then, again: *Robin!*

11.

But Robin didn't come.

Oh, for Heaven's sake, said Charlotte, drying her hands on a kitchen towel, and went out into the yard.

Once she was there she realized, with a slight unease that was more irritation than anything else, that she had no idea where to look. His bicycle was leaning against the porch. He knew not to wander off so close to dinnertime, especially when they had company.

Robin! she called. Was he hiding? No children his age lived in the neighborhood, and though every now and then unkempt children—black and white—wandered up from the river to the wide, oak-shaded sidewalks of George Street, she didn't see any of them now. Ida forbade him to play with them, though sometimes he did anyway. The smallest ones were pitiful, with their scabbed knees and dirty feet; though Ida Rhew shooed them roughly from the yard, Charlotte, in tender-hearted moods, sometimes gave them quarters or glasses of lemonade. But when they grew older—thirteen or fourteen—she was glad to retreat into the house and allow Ida to be as fierce as she liked in chasing them away. They shot BB guns at dogs, stole things from people's porches, used bad language, and ran the streets till all hours of the night.

Ida said: Some of them trashy little boys was running down the street a while ago.

When Ida said trashy, she meant white. Ida hated the poor white children and blamed them with unilateral ferocity for all yard mishaps, even those with which Charlotte was certain they could have had nothing possibly to do.

Was Robin with them? said Charlotte.

Nome.

Where are they now?

I run them off.

Which way?

Yunder towards the depot.

Old Mrs. Fountain from next door, in her white cardigan and harlequin glasses, had come out into her yard to see what was happening. Close behind was her decrepit poodle, Mickey, with whom she shared a comical resemblance: sharp nose, stiff gray curls, suspicious thrust of chin.

Well, she called gaily. Yall having a big party over there?

Just the family, Charlotte called back, scanning the darkening horizon behind Natchez Street where the train tracks stretched flat in the distance. She should have invited Mrs. Fountain to dinner. Mrs. Fountain was a widow, and her only child had died in the

Figure |8-19|

Novels present readers with linear reading—a situation in which a single column is adequate. Novels are also designed with a reader's comfort in mind. In the case of *The Little Friend*, margins are wide enough to allow room for fingers to hold the book without covering text. Kidd chose to place folios at the top of the page rather than at the bottom so they would be easy for readers to spot.

this murder mystery even though the title sounded more like the title of a children's book. Luck and inspiration struck when he encountered an antique baby mannequin head at a friend's home. After having the mannequin head photographed, Kidd cropped it in ways that exploited its potential for creating a sense of mystery and apprehension.

Annual Reports

Annual reports serve corporations by giving shareholders and other supporters an idea of how the company has performed. Corporations that are publicly owned are obligated to publish and distribute an annual report to all of its stockholders; the Federal Security and Exchange Commission mandates this. Those that are not publicly owned often publish annual reports to give financial backers, clients and other interested parties information on the nature of their business and how successful it has been. Annual reports are typically issued at the beginning of a calendar year and report on the company's financial performance over the past year. Some of the information that annual reports contain include data on corporate sales and profits as well as the corporation's stock value.

Although annual reports need to include business facts and figures, they should also send a message that the company is on sound financial footing. Annual reports typically include a letter from the CEO to assure its customers and shareholders that a company's future is in good hands, as well as other information that communicates a positive impression of the company's products and services.

Example: *Fossil 2002 Annual Report*

Fossil is perhaps best known for its flagship product, FOSSIL brand watches, which are sold in department stores and other retail establishments. The company's other watch brands and products, which include jewelry and accessories, are distinguished by their unique fashion details and creative touches, as well as innovative packaging. An in-house creative team coordinates Fossil's product design, packaging, advertising, and in-store promotion to communicate a cohesive brand philosophy.

Because fashion plays such an important role in Fossil's mission, it was important for Fossil's 2002 annual report to exude fashion, as well as an awareness of youthful fashion trends. An important part of the Fossil brand has also been built on "retro" looks. The Fossil design team chose to capitalize on a resurgence of 1970's fashions with their design of Fossil's 2002 annual report.

Figure |8-20|

The annual report's cover hints at its 1970s "retro" theme with stripes in a color palette that is evocative of the era.

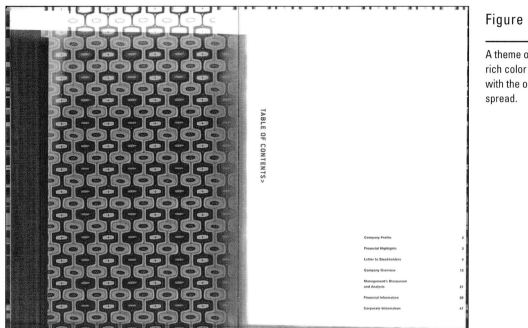

Figure | 8-21 |

A theme of pattern and rich color is established with the opening spread.

COMPANY PROFILE

Fossil is a design, development, marketing and distribution company that specializes in consumer products predicated on fashion and value. The Company's principal offerings include an extensive line of fashion watches sold under the Company's proprietary FOSSIL®, RELIC® and ZODIAC® brands as well as licensed brands for some of the most prestigious companies in the world, including EMPORIO ARMANI®, DKNY®, DIESEL® and BURBERRY®. The Company also offers complementary lines of small leather goods, belts, handbags and sunglasses under the FOSSIL and RELIC brands, jewelry under the FOSSIL and EMPORIO ARMANI brands and FOSSIL apparel. The Company's products are sold in department stores and specialty retail stores in over 90 countries around the world, in addition to the Company's e-commerce website at www.fossil.com.

The Company differentiates its products from those of its competitors principally through innovations in fashion details. These innovations include variations in the treatment of watch dials, crystals, cases, straps and bracelets for the Company's watches and innovative treatments and details in its other accessories. An in-house creative services team coordinates product design, packaging, advertising and in-store presentations to more effectively and cohesively communicate to its target markets the themes and images associated with its brands. Brand name development is further enhanced through Company-owned stores as well as the Company's website.

Utilizing several wholly and majority-owned watch assembly facilities and centralized distribution points enables the Company to reduce its inventory risk, increase flexibility in meeting the delivery requirements of its customers and maintain significant cost advantages compared to its competitors. Additionally, the Company's centralized infrastructure in development/design coupled with its production/sourcing capabilities allows it to leverage the strength of its branded watch portfolio over an extensive global distribution network.

NET SALES
(in millions of dollars)

OPERATING INCOME
(in millions of dollars)

NET INCOME
(in millions of dollars)

STOCKHOLDERS' EQUITY
(in millions of dollars)

FINANCIAL HIGHLIGHTS

| Fiscal Year | 2002 | 2001 | 2000 | 1999 | 1998 |
IN THOUSANDS, EXCEPT PER SHARE DATA					
Net sales	$ 663,338	$ 545,541	$ 504,285	$ 418,762	$ 304,743
Gross profit	334,085	271,850	255,746	212,687	150,504
Operating income	95,930	76,854	93,621	97,449	55,370
Income before income taxes	95,979	72,804	94,717	87,841	54,729
Net income	58,907	43,683 (1)	55,883	51,826	32,161
Earnings per share: (2)					
Basic	1.28	0.97 (1)	1.18	1.08	0.69
Diluted	1.22	0.93 (1)	1.14	1.03	0.66
Weighted average common shares outstanding: (2)					
Basic	45,993	45,251	47,534	47,850	46,581
Diluted	48,238	46,860	49,013	50,142	48,879
Working capital	$ 241,177	$ 163,290	$ 169,792	$ 155,198	$ 109,040
Total assets	482,526	380,863	307,591	269,364	194,078
Long-term debt	–	–	–	–	–
Stockholders' equity	340,541	264,023	220,699	191,197	134,919
Return on average stockholders' equity	19.9 %	18.3%	26.9 %	32.2 %	29.3 %

(1) Includes a $2.9 million one-time charge which reflects the write-off of the carrying value of the Company's investment in SII Marketing International, Inc. as a result of the Company's decision to terminate its equity participation in the joint venture relationship. Excluding this one-time charge, pro forma net income, basic earnings per share and diluted earnings per share were $46.5 million, $1.03 and $0.99, respectively.
(2) All share and per share price data has been adjusted to reflect three-for-two stock splits effected in the form of a stock dividend paid on August 17, 1999 and June 7, 2002.

STOCK INFORMATION

The Company's common stock prices are published daily in The Wall Street Journal and other publications under the NASDAQ National Market Listing. The stock is traded under the ticker symbol "FOSL." The following are the high and low sale prices of the Company's stock per the NASDAQ National Market. All share price data has been adjusted to reflect a three-for-two stock split effected in the form of a stock dividend paid on June 7, 2002. Stock prices have been adjusted in certain cases to the nearest traded amount.

| | 2002 | | 2001 | |
	High	Low	High	Low
First quarter	$ 18.667	$ 13.167	$ 13.500	$ 9.167
Second quarter	23.740	17.527	15.567	11.007
Third quarter	24.610	15.600	14.867	9.407
Fourth quarter	22.620	14.990	16.067	10.767

As of March 28, 2003, the Company estimates that there were approximately 6,000 beneficial owners of the Company's Common Stock, represented by approximately 160 holders of record.

Dividend Policy. The Company expects that it will retain all available earnings generated by its operations for the development and growth of its business and does not anticipate paying any cash dividends in the foreseeable future. Any future determination as to dividend policy will be made in the discretion of the Board of Directors of the Company and will depend on a number of factors, including the future earnings, capital requirements, financial condition and future prospects of the Company and such other factors as the Board of Directors may deem relevant.

2/3

Figure | 8-22 |

The company's profile and financial highlights pages are some of the simplest and most straightforward in the annual report. Consistent typography and charts colored with hues from the annual report's palette help these pages tie in with the rest of the publication.

Figure | 8-23 |

A letter to stockholders from the company CEO is a standard part of any annual report. Although this page is more conservatively designed than others, the application of pattern and layered imagery helps it blend with the annual report's other pages.

Figure | 8-24 |

Fossil's global presence is emphasized on a spread that features photographs of international landmarks. The repetition of the photographs creates a sense of pattern that mimics other pattern applications throughout the annual report.

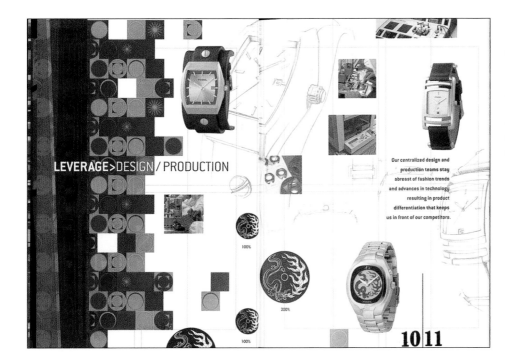

Figure |8-25|

Even though imagery
and content vary with
every page, the use of
pattern, consistent
typography, and colors
tie the annual report's
various pages together.

Promotional Literature

Promotional literature exists to raise awareness and interest in the minds of its readers. Whereas publications that entertain or inform their readers place an emphasis on making content reader accessible, promotional literature places a priority on creating an impression. Although readers may be getting information that raises their awareness, they are more likely to react if they are responding on an emotional as well as an intellectual level. Designers of promotional literature recognize this emotional aspect and base their design strategy on eliciting an emotional as well as an intellectual response from their audience.

Publications that promote can be selling services, merchandise, a brand, a concept, an organization, or an individual. Unlike the other types of publications that have been presented in this chapter, promotional literature is open ended in its design and usually presents designers with more freedom and flexibility than other types of literature. Format, visual approach, and other aspects are all guided by the publication's promotional goal.

Example: Cher Tour Book

Like most concert tour books, *Living Proof* is a pictorial essay full of photographs and meaningful quotes; however, this tour book goes beyond most in its scope and design. To commemorate Cher's Farewell Tour, Margo Chase Design was hired to create a tour book that paid tribute to Cher's incredible career—one that has spanned four decades. The firm's design for the 36-page book serves as a testament to Cher's superstar status and staying power in its ability to vividly depict the musical artist during memorable periods in rock history. The design

Figure |8-26|

The tour book cover features Cher as she looks today and an iconic
Cher logo designed by Margo Chase Design.

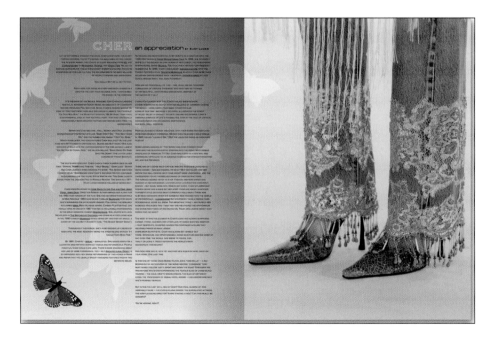

Figure |8-27|

The book's opening spread features a tribute to Cher and continues the blue color scheme and butterfly
motif established with the cover.

Figure | 8-28 |

A "retro" color palette, typographic treatment, and other graphic effects that simulate the look of 1960s rock posters and album cover design distinguish the title page of the 1960s section from other sections in the book.

Figure | 8-29 |

Each section of the tour book contains photos from a specific era, in this case, photos of Cher from the 1960s.

Figure |8-30|

Although the typography, color, and stylistic treatments vary from one decade to the next, the repetition of geometric shapes and silhouetted photographs help unify the spreads.

accomplishes this by employing graphic treatments and stylistic techniques that capture the spirit of rock and pop culture in each of four decades: the 1960s, 1970s, 1980s, and 1990s. The tour book also celebrates Cher's outspoken persona and distinctive style. It became a treasured memento for fans who purchased it at her Farewell Concert.

SUMMARY

Magazines are published on a regular basis and are frequently targeted at a specific demographic, special interest, or trade group. Most magazine formats include a table of contents, departments and columns, and a feature section. Newspapers are usually published on a daily basis and target a broad audience. They are unbound and are broken down into sections where the section with the most newsworthy content is wrapped around other sections. Newspapers are typically text heavy and typographically driven. Typographic hierarchy is created by varying the weight and scale of the type. Newsletters are similar to newspapers and magazines but on a much smaller scale. They have fewer pages, limited distribution, and a smaller budget. Book design places a lot of emphasis on the

Figure | 8-30 |

Continued from page 183.

cover or jacket. Book covers can be image-driven or typographically driven. A book's interior design typically includes a title page, table of contents, and chapters. Books vary in the amount of imagery they include. Because of their long shelf life, time and care go into every detail of a book's design. Annual reports are published to give shareholders and financial backers information on a company's performance. They typically include a letter from the CEO and information on a company's stock value and financial performance. Promotional literature is designed to raise interest and awareness among readers by creating an impression; its primary goal is to create an emotional response rather than to inform.

in review

1. What type of publication is frequently used to reach a narrow demographic?

2. What is the function of a magazine's masthead?

3. Why is typographic hierarchy important in a newspaper?

4. How do newsletters differ from magazines and newspapers?

5. What visual components are part of a book's cover or jacket design?

6. How does an annual report serve a corporation and its shareholders?

projects

Project Title Magazine Redesign

Project Brief Find an existing magazine that you feel could benefit from a new design and redesign it using the existing copy and visuals. Use your understanding of color, typography, imagery, and design principles to come up with a new design concept that does a better job of visually communicating the magazine's goal and attracting its intended audience. The redesign should consist of a new cover, table of contents, a department page, and a feature spread.

Objectives

Simulate the experience of developing a magazine design.

Design within a format common to most magazines.

Create a concept for typography, a color palette, imagery treatment, and a grid that supports a magazine's communication goal.

Understand how theme and variation works by creating a unified design for pages with different editorial functions.

Project Title Endangered Species Brochure

Project Brief Create a publication that promotes the protection of an endangered species of animal. The publication needs to inform others of the plight of this species, as well as communicate the physical characteristics and essence of the animal and its habitat. It must also intrigue its audience enough to invite closer inspection. Pick a format, paper type, and binding method that work to achieve these two objectives. You may incorporate decorative cuts and unusual materials to help achieve these objectives. Text and visuals can be original art or photography or borrowed from outside sources.

Objectives

Gain experience designing a publication that promotes a cause.

Develop a design that elicits an emotional reaction in its readers.

Design a publication that exploits hierarchy, dimensionality, and layering to intrigue readers.

Communicate an impression that gives a sense of the publication's subject matter.

Encourage creative freedom in the design and the development of a promotional brochure.

notes

┃ professional opportunities in publication design ┃

g

objectives

Understand the general qualifications and demands common to most publication design jobs.

Appreciate and learn about the differences between specialized areas of publication design.

Know the variety of roles designers can assume in publication design.

Learn about the work and careers of successful publication design professionals.

introduction

Publication designers enhance the written word, adding nuance and clarity to editorial content. Because they give visual form to content, publication designers are often required to read it or, at the very least, have a thorough understanding of a publication's content. If you are contemplating a career in publication design, it helps to have a love of the written word.

Because publication designers get intensively involved in working with words, it is also helpful to have an understanding of written language, including a basic knowledge of grammar, spelling, word usage, and sentence structure. A thorough knowledge of typography and a flair for working with type is also an asset.

Publication designers are often responsible for finding photography and illustration to support editorial content. This requires working with image suppliers such as stock agencies as well as contracting with other creative professionals. Publication designers also work with editors, authors, and marketing executives. In this role, and in managing the large volume of work and variety of components involved in any publication, they need to function as effective managers. It helps to be a team player and have good organization and managerial skills.

The aforementioned attributes are common to most design jobs in the publishing industry. However, there are variances between different areas of publishing and the roles designers assume in these areas. This chapter explores the design jobs that exist in publishing and how they differ from each other.

Magazine/Editorial Design

Magazine designers have responsibility for a magazine's overall design as well as the design of the editorial content for each issue. Let us look first at the responsibility of developing a magazine's basic design.

The design of most magazines is based on standards that have been established to support the publication's goal. These standards include the magazine's logo design as well as the format, grid, typography, color palette, and other design and stylistic attributes upon which a magazine's design is based. Although each issue is unique, these underlying standards or rules govern the design of each issue so there is visual continuity from one issue to the next. The individual who is responsible for the magazine's design establishes these guidelines. It is not unusual for the art director or designer in this role to seek assistance from an outside designer or design firm to gain objectivity or special expertise. In this respect, some designers and design firms specialize as publication design consultants.

After a magazine's overall design has been established, templates and style guides are established for its various pages. The templates are created with software designed specifically for publication layout. The magazine's grid and type specifications are included in the template to serve as a guide for the design and production of each issue. A printed style manual is often produced to provide additional information and ensure continuity in the design of each issue.

CAREER PROFILE

Fred Woodward

As a college student in the 1970s, Fred Woodward was undecided about his future. He switched majors from journalism, to physical education, to political science before settling on graphic design at Memphis State University. His final choice was fortuitous. A short time after switching into graphic design, he landed a job at a Memphis-based design firm, which led to a position as art director of *Memphis*, a regional magazine.

After working for *Memphis*, Woodward served as art director at a succession of regional magazines including Dallas' *D Magazine* and *Texas Monthly*. After leaving *Texas Monthly* in 1987, Woodward became art director of *Rolling Stone*, the venerable bible of rock and roll. In this role, Woodward spent 14 years continuing the magazine's tradition of celebrating colorful celebrities and subject matter with innovative illustration, photography, and design. Woodward's most recent endeavor has been design director of *GQ*, which won a Magazine of the Year award from the Society of Publication Designers after just 1 year under his direction.

Woodward has also won countless national and regional awards and in 1996 was inducted into the Art Director's Hall of Fame. In 2004, he received The American Institute of Graphic Arts Medal for lifetime achievement, the highest honor the profession bestows.

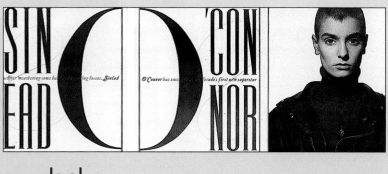

Figure |9-2|

Many of Woodward's innovative designs for *Rolling Stone* used large-scale type in unusual ways. In this layout, it appears on two pages as a dramatic counterpoint to a full-page photograph.

Figure |9-3|

In his current role as design director for *Gentleman's Quarterly*, Woodward was intensively involved in the magazine's redesign. His flair for working creatively with type is timeless, as evidenced in the contemporary look of this feature spread.

A magazine's design staff can consist of one individual or many. It is not unusual for a small magazine to be completely designed by one individual, who develops its basic design and then implements it from one issue to the next. Larger magazines may have a staff of several designers with a hierarchy established between their roles. The individual with the most responsibility, often the creative or art director, oversees the design and production of each issue and has responsibility for the overall design of a magazine. Other staff designers take responsibility for the design and layout of departments and columns as well as the editorial feature section. Magazine designers rarely take on responsibility for designing the ads that go into a magazine, but are responsible for designing the editorial content that appears on pages that include advertising.

As discussed in Chapter Eight, magazines often exist to serve specific audiences or special interest groups. Designers involved with a magazine often have an affinity for or interest in the magazine's subject matter, a factor that often helps them bring additional understanding and passion to their design.

Newspaper Design

Newspaper designers perform many of the same tasks and take on similar responsibilities as magazine designers. Designing a newspaper is a time-consuming process that may involve other designers who are brought in as consultants. Newspaper design involves selecting typefaces and determining a grid struc-

CAREER PROFILE

Mario Garcia

Mario R. Garcia is chief executive officer (CEO) and Founder of Garcia Media, a Tampa, FL–based design consultancy specializing in newspaper redesign. Trained as a journalist, Garcia is committed to the idea that writing, editing, and design must all work together for effective communication. Although he majored in journalism and began his career as a journalist, Garcia soon realized he was drawn to layout design, a process he describes as ``visual journalism.'' Garcia formed Garcia media in 1996, but has been a newspaper designer/consultant for 35 years, during which time he has consulted with more than 500 newspapers from all over the world, large and small, including the *Wall Street Journal, Hdelsblatt and Die Zeit*, and *Newsday*.

Garcia also has many years of teaching experience as a journalism professor at Miami-Dade

Community College and as a professor of graphic arts at Syracuse University's Newhouse School of Public Communications and the University of South Florida. A frequent lecturer at universities in 14 countries, in addition to the United States, Garcia has also served as an organizer and moderator for countless seminars on communication, journalism, and newspaper design.

Figure | 9-5 |

Garcia Media's redesign of the *San Francisco Examiner* reconfigured the paper from a broadsheet to tabloid format. The new format is a more convenient size for reading on a bus, train, or trolley. Other features of the new design include a major revamping of the sports section and color-aided navigational devices that make information easy for readers to find.

ture as well as a plan for imagery. Like magazines, a newspaper's design standards are developed into templates and style guides which are published in a standards manual that serves as a reference for everyone involved in its design and production. A newspaper's design standards are likely to be based on high legibility and ease of reading. Because newspapers are designed and produced on a tight schedule, they are also designed with quick and flexible production in mind.

As mentioned in Chapter Eight, newspapers are broken down into sections. An art director and designer are typically responsible for the design and layout of each section, including commissioning illustration or photography. Although the design of a newspaper's sections is based on consistent design standards, each section reflects the distinctive style of its design team. Sections that deal with breaking news are designed very quickly on a daily basis. In the case of some sections, such as those devoted to lifestyle, many features are planned in advance, allowing designers enough lead time to commission illustration and photography. Weekly sections dealing with entertainment, travel, or other topics allow even more lead time.

The newsroom is an exciting place to work. The energy involved in changing and adapting a publication as stories develop creates a fast-paced work environment. Designers who like to be on top of current events and adapt readily to quick changes and a high-key work pace will enjoy newspaper design.

CAREER PROFILE

Louise Fili

Louise Fili's work reflects a love of typography that was cultivated early in her life when she worked as a student in her college's type shop. Her typographic and design skills were further developed while working as a senior designer from 1976 to 1978 for the legendary Herb Lubalin. In 1978, Fili became the art director of Pantheon Books where she designed more than 2000 book jackets. Some of her most noteworthy designs for Pantheon reflect a fascination with typography from the early twentieth century as well as French and Italian period looks. Vacations in Europe during the summer offered Fili a chance to visit flea markets and used book stores where she found a wealth of inspiring material. Fili applied a fresh eye to evocative book jacket designs that incorporate many of the antique typefaces and photographic techniques that intrigued her.

Fili left Pantheon to form her own firm in 1989. Louise Fili Ltd. specializes in logo, package, restaurant type, book, and book jacket design. She has won awards from many major design competitions including gold and silver medals from The Society of Illustrators and the New York Art Directors Club. Fili's work is also in the permanent collections of the Library of Congress, the Cooper Hewitt Museum, and the Biblithéque Nationale. Fili was recently inducted into the Art Directors Hall of Fame.

Figure |9-7|

Fili's 1985 cover design for *The Lover,* with its vignetted photo and shadowed Art Deco-era typography, reflects her love of vintage looks.

Figure |9-8|

Euro Deco, a book Fili coauthored with Steven Heller, also features a cover she designed.

Figure |9-9|

Fili's design expertise extends into logo design for restaurants, food packaging and other brands and businesses. (see below)

Figure |9-9| (cont.)

Book Design

Book design is often broken down into two parts: (1) the design of the book cover or jacket and (2) the design of the interior. Book designers can do both, or they can specialize in one of these areas.

Book design and publishing falls into many special categories and can be broken down into several main areas: children's books, trade publications, textbooks, fiction/nonfiction, and special interest (cookbooks, gardening, travel, and so on). Each niche is unique in the kind of design expertise it requires.

Children's Books

Because young children need picture books to help them read, publishers specializing in children's books place a high priority on illustration. Designers in this area work with illustrators to develop page layouts that allow text and imagery to work synergistically. In fact, it is not uncommon for the illustrator to determine where text will fall on a page. Children's book designers advise and assist in this process, and select typography suitable to the book and its audience. They typically take responsibility for the book's cover design.

Trade Publications and Textbooks

Trade publications and textbooks are published for audiences seeking specific information or expertise. Although the cover design is important, its role is not as critical as it would be in a more competitive retail environment.

One of the key factors for designers of these books is the need to make information easy to read and accessible. The interior design must help readers navigate and understand what they are reading. Designers typically take on responsibility for all aspects of the design, including interior and cover design, but they may commission illustrators, photographers, and other freelancers to assist them in cover development and other aspects of a book's development.

Designers who specialize in this type of work are often part of an in-house design department involving an art director and one or several designers. Publishers vary widely in the way they handle the design and production of their books. Some publishers commission an outside designer to develop a basic design for a book. When the design has been established, a template and style guides are given to the in-house design team to use in the layout of the book. Other publishers let their design department make the decision on bringing in outside expertise.

Fiction/Nonfiction

Publishers of these books are involved in the production and mass marketing of thousands of titles every year, including best sellers. Effective cover design is crucial in this incredibly competitive publishing arena. Design responsibilities are often separated in a company, with an art director or designer taking responsibility for covers, while another assumes responsibility for interior design.

Publishers of fiction and nonfiction titles generally break down their projects into two divisions: (1) trade books, those that are issued in hardback, and (2) mass market or paperback books. The deadlines involved in the design of trade books are usually more generous than those for paperbacks. Art directors and designers of trade book covers, which are often book jackets, are intensively involved with marketing executives, editors, and the book's author in the development of a design. They often commission photographers and illustrators to assist them with the development of a cover concept, but are ultimately responsible for its layout and typography. Mass market or paperback books are handled similarly, but the art director or designer is often less encumbered by the need to develop a design that pleases many other individuals. In many cases, a paperback cover involves reconfiguring an existing design that first appeared on a book's jacket.

The number of designers involved in any book jacket or cover design and whether they work in-house or as freelancers depends on the size of the company and the preferences of its art director or designer. Sometimes a single art director may take on responsibility for designing hundreds of titles per year and commission freelancers to assist. In other situations, an art director may work with an in-house design team and limit freelancers to illustrators and photographers.

Special Interest

Publishers of special interest books deal with a wide range of topics. Special interest books exist to serve gourmets, cooks, cat lovers, gardeners, surfers, classic car enthusiasts, stamp collectors, and many types of hobbyists. The list could go on endlessly! In each case, the book's design must support its subject matter as well as capture and reflect a spirit that will engage its audience of enthusiasts. Because many of these books are sold in a competitive retail environment, cover design is as critical as it would be for a trade book. The book's interior design is also an important factor. Most special interest books feature a combination of text and imagery, although the proportion of text to imagery varies depending on the subject matter. Art directors and designers of these books tend to take responsibility for both interior and cover design, using support staff or freelancers to assist them.

Catalog Design

As our lives have become busier and busier, more and more consumers are turning to catalogs as a way of maximizing their time by purchasing items through the mail. The high quality of the merchandise sold through the mail and the catalogs featuring this merchandise has given new status and credibility to catalogs as an opportunity for designers.

Creating consumer desire and initiating the purchase of goods is critical in this area of publication design where designers are often as much involved in brand design as they are in publication design. Catalog designers often work with retail executives and fashion experts in developing an overall design and look for the retailer or brand they represent. They also work intensively with photographers in presenting merchandise in the most attractive and desirable way possible.

Catalog designers are often part of an in-house team involving writers and other production personnel who develop other aspects of a retailer's print and web promotion. However, catalog design is not exclusively the domain of in-house designers. There are many instances in which a catalog's design is entirely developed or assisted by an outside design firm specializing in retail promotion.

CAREER PROFILE

Robert Valentine

Robert Valentine founded The Valentine Group, his New York City-based design firm, in 1991 after holding creative management positions with Bloomingdales in New York City, as well as Dayton Hudson and Donaldson's Department Store in Minneapolis. His design firm specializes in branding, rebranding, advertising, and identity campaigns for fashion and retail brands such as Neiman Marcus, William-Sonoma, J. Crew, and Sundance.

Although much of Valentine's career and expertise has its roots in fashion retail, he has also attained prominence as a publication designer. Much of his knowledge of design for the fashion and retailing has been applied to catalog design. Valentine has even authored a book, *Catalog Design: The Art of Creating Desire*, which focuses on outstanding catalog design. He often serves as a consultant to magazine design and editorial staffs seeking his expertise on design and redesign

Valentine's other accomplishments in publication design include books and magazines. He helped develop and launch *Real Simple*, one of the most successful consumer magazines in recent history. Valentine was also involved in the design of *Martha Stewart Living* during its infancy and recently was involved in the redesign and relaunch of *STEP inside design* magazine. Valentine has won many regional and national awards. His work is part of the permanent collections of several museums, including the Cooper Hewitt and the Smithsonian.

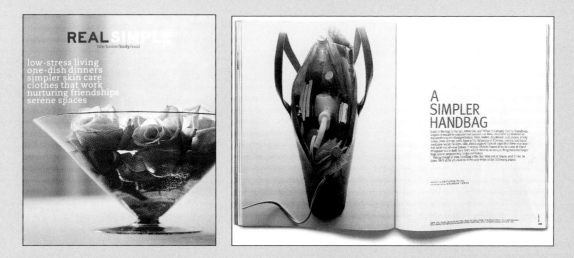

Figure |9-11|

Valentine's involvement in the design of *Real Simple* included designing the magazine's logo and selecting fonts that give the magazine its clean, no-nonsense look. Valentine's concept also features airy layouts that incorporate lots of white space.

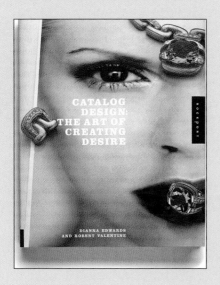

Figure |9-12|

Catalog Design: The Art of Creating Desire is a book featuring outstanding catalog design for fashion and home furnishings. In addition to co-authoring the book, Valentine and his firm designed the book's cover and interior layouts.

VOLUME 18 NUMBER 4

STEP
INSIDE DESIGN

STEPSTEPSTEPSTEPSTEPSTEP

www.stepinsidedesign.com

PREMIER ISSUE
the world of design from the inside out

BEYOND THE GLOSS *with* christopher griffith
paula scher | robert valentine | cathie bleck
tobias frere-jones | jonathan hoefler
gary baseman *and more*

| glossary |

Additive color: Color as projected light. The additive color system is based on the additive primaries of red, green and blue (RGB).

Basis weight: In the US and Canada, the weight, in pounds, of a ream (500 sheets) of paper cut to basic size.

Bit map: *See* **Line art.**

Bleed: A printed area that extends beyond the trimmed edge of a printed piece.

Body text: Body of written content on a page or document. Also called body copy or text.

Bulking dummy: Sheets of a selected paper, bound in the specified number of pages and trimmed to size, to simulate how a publication will look and feel before it is printed.

Caption: A word, phrase of sentence placed close to a photograph or illustration as a means of identifying or describing it. Also called a cutline.

Character: All items on the keyboard, including letters of the alphabet, numbers and punctuation marks, that are part of a font.

Centered: Text or lines of type centered on a central vertical axis.

CMYK: Color system widely used in the graphic arts industry and related software as a means of designating four-color process.

Column: Blocks of type or text set at the same width.

Continuous tone image: Photograph or illustration that's comprised of a series of gray or color tones with gradations from one tone or color to the next.

Cuneiform: Early form of written communication that involved inscribing symbols on clay, stone, metal and other hard materials.

Cutline: See caption.

Deck: A phrase, sentence or several sentences that appear in close proximity to the title of a story or article. Also called a lead-in.

Demographic: A statistical sampling of the human population.

Display ads: Printed advertising that takes up a full page in a publication.

Feature section: Editorial content, uninterrupted by advertising, that appears in the center of a publication.

Flush left/ragged right: Type or text aligned to a left vertical axis that is uneven on the right.

Flush right/ragged left: Type or text aligned to a right vertical axis that is uneven on the left.

Focal point: Visual element with the most emphasis in a layout or composition.

Font: A complete set of letterforms (uppercase and lowercase), numerals, and punctuation marks in a particular typeface that allows for typesetting by keystroke on a computer or other means of typographic composition.

Four-color system, four-color process: Method of printing that uses cyan, magenta, yellow, and black to reproduce full-color images. Also called CMYK.

Fractional ads: Printed advertising that takes up a portion of a page.

Full bleed: A printed area that extends beyond all edges of a printed piece.

Golden mean: A harmonic arrangement or proportion system that has been found in plants and other life forms.

Grayscale image: A continuous tone black-and-white image.

Grid: An underlying structure or a transparent framework for determining where to align graphic elements, imagery and text in a page layout.

Gutter: Gap between columns of text in a page layout or between pages in a spread.

Halftone reproduction: Reproducing a continuous-tone image by photographing it through a fine screen to convert the image into a series of dots.

Headline: An article title set in large type so that it has prominence on a page.

Hieroglyphics: A series of pictures used as written communication in ancient Egypt.

High-key: Light in value.

Justified: Text or lines of type aligned to both left and right sides.

Kern: Selectively adjusting letterspacing between the letters of a word.

Illuminated manuscripts: Elaborate and highly detailed books that combined words and images with decorative letterforms.

Initial cap: A technique where the first letter of the first word at the beginning of a paragraph is made larger than surrounding text.

Layout: A composed page or cover design.

Lead-in: (See deck).

Leading: The amount of vertical space between lines of type.

Letterform: The particular style and form of each individual letter in an alphabet.

Letterpress: A process of printing from an inked, raised surface.

Letter spacing: Modifying the distance between the letters in a word. Also called tracking.

Line art: A black-and-white image that does not have continuos tones. Also called **Bitmap.**

Line length: Horizontal length of a line of type.

Line of golden proportion: A means of creating harmonic proportion based on dividing a page into eighths.

Lithography: Process of printing from a flat surface that has been treated so that the image area is ink receptive and the non-image area is ink repellent.

Lowercase: Smaller letters, as opposed to capital letters, of a type font.

Low-key: Dark in value.

Margin: White space at the top, bottom. and to the left and eight of a body of type.

Master page: Page template with a column grid and margins in place.

Offset lithography: Most commonly used method of printing where an image on a plate is "offset" into a rubber blanket cylinder which, in turn, transfers the image to a sheet of paper.

Orphan: A piece of a word or word left by itself at the end of a line or a column of text. Also called **Widow.**

Outlining: Isolating a photographic subject or other image from its background. Also called silhouetting.

Point: A unit used for measuring the height of type and vertical distance between lines of type.

Points of entry: Graphic elements that catch a reader's attention and lead them further into editorial content.

Process color: Inks used in four-color process printing: cyan, magenta, yellow, and black.

Pull quote: A direct quote from an article or story that is set apart and placed prominently in the article or story layout.

Rivers: Unsightly areas of white space that occur in justified columns where spaces between words are unusually wide.

Sans serif: Typefaces without serifs or brackets.

Script: A typographic style that simulates the look of calligraphy, hand writing or hand lettering.

Serif: Typefaces with serifs or brackets.

Shades: The mix of black with a color.

Sidebar: Editorial content that is sectioned off from the body of an article or story so that it stands apart as supplementary information.

Silhouetting: *See* **Outlining.**

Spread: Two facing pages in a layout.

Subhead: Typographic treatment of a word or series of words that identify editorial content.

Subtractive color: Color as mixed pigment. The subtractive color system is based on the subtractive primaries of red, blue and yellow.

Symbols: An image that stands for something else.

Tint: The mix of white with a color.

Tracking: See letter spacing.

Type alignment: Aligning lines of type or text to an imaginary axis.

Typeface: The design of a single set of letterforms, numerals, and punctuation marks unified by consistent visuals properties.

Typestyle: Modifications in a typeface that create design variety while maintaining the visual character of the typeface. These include variations in weight, width or angle.

Type family: A range of style variations based on a single typeface design.

Uppercase: The capital or large letters of a type font.

Widow: A piece of a word or word left by itself at the end of a line or a column of text. Also called **Orphan.**

FOSSIL >2002 ANNUAL REPORT

subject index

*Page numbers followed by **b** indicate boxes; page numbers followed by f indicate figures; page numbers followed by **t** indicate tables.*